Resilience and Reliability on AWS

Jurg van Vliet, Flavia Paganelli, and Jasper Geurtsen

O'REILLY®

Beijing · Cambridge · Farnham · Köln · Sebastopol · Tokyo

Resilience and Reliability on AWS

by Jurg van Vliet, Flavia Paganelli, and Jasper Geurtsen

Published by O'Reilly Media, Inc., 1005 Gravenstein Highway North, Sebastopol, CA 95472.

O'Reilly books may be purchased for educational, business, or sales promotional use. Online editions are also available for most titles (*http://my.safaribooksonline.com*). For more information, contact our corporate/institutional sales department: 800-998-9938 or *corporate@oreilly.com*.

Editors: Mike Loukides and Meghan Blanchette	**Proofreader:** Mary Ellen Smith
Production Editor: Rachel Steely	**Cover Designer:** Karen Montgomery
	Interior Designer: David Futato
	Illustrator: Rebecca Demarest

January 2013:   First Edition

Revision History for the First Edition:

2012-12-21   First release

See *http://oreilly.com/catalog/errata.csp?isbn=9781449339197* for release details.

ISBN: 978-1-449-33919-7

[LSI]

Table of Contents

Foreword

In mid-2008, I was handling operations for reddit.com, an online community for sharing and discussing links, serving a few tens of millions of page views per month. At the time, we were hosting the whole site on 21 1U HP servers (in addition to four of the original servers for the site) in two racks in a San Francisco data center. Around that time, Steve, one of the founders of reddit, came to me and suggested I check out this AWS thing that his buddies at Justin.tv (*http://www.justin.tv*) had been using with some success; he thought it might be good for us, too. I set up a VPN; we copied over a set of our data, and started using it for batch processing.

In early 2009, we had a problem: we needed more servers for live traffic, so we had to make a choice—build out another rack of servers, or move to AWS. We chose the latter, partly because we didn't know what our growth was going to look like, and partly because it gave us enormous flexibility for resiliency and redundancy by offering multiple availability zones, as well as multiple regions if we ever got to that point. Also, I was tired of running to the data center every time a disk failed, a fan died, a CPU melted, etc.

When designing any architecture, one of the first assumptions one should make is that any part of the system can break at any time. AWS is no exception. Instead of fearing this failure, one must embrace it. At reddit, one of the things we got right with AWS from the start was making sure that we had copies of our data in at least two zones. This proved handy during the great EBS outage of 2011. While we were down for a while, it was for a lot less time than most sites, in large part because we were able to spin up our databases in the other zone, where we kept a second copy of all of our data. If not for that, we would have been down for over a day, like all the other sites in the same situation.

During that EBS outage, I, like many others, watched Netflix (*http://www.netflix.com*), also hosted on AWS. It is said that if you're on AWS and your site is down, but Netflix is up, it's probably your fault you are down. It was that reputation, among other things, that drew me to move from reddit to Netflix, which I did in July 2011. Now that I'm responsible for Netflix's uptime, it is my job to help the company maintain that reputation.

Netflix requires a superior level of reliability. With tens of thousands of instances and 30 million plus paying customers, reliability is absolutely critical. So how do we do it? We expect the inevitable failure, plan for it, and even cause it sometimes. At Netflix, we follow our monkey theory—we simulate things that go wrong and find things that are different. And thus was born the Simian Army, our collection of agents that constructively muck with our AWS environment to make us more resilient to failure.

The most famous of these is the Chaos Monkey, which kills random instances in our production account—the same account that serves actual, live customers. Why wait for Amazon to fail when you can induce the failure yourself, right? We also have the Latency Monkey, which induces latency on connections between services to simulate network issues. We have a whole host of other monkeys too (most of them available on Github).

The point of the Monkeys is to make sure we are ready for any failure modes. Sometimes it works, and we avoid outages, and sometimes new failures come up that we haven't planned for. In those cases, our resiliency systems are truly tested, making sure they are generic and broad enough to handle the situation.

One failure that we weren't prepared for was in June 2012. A severe storm hit Amazon's complex in Virginia, and they lost power to one of their data centers (a.k.a. Availability Zones). Due to a bug in the mid-tier load balancer that we wrote, we did not route traffic away from the affected zone, which caused a cascading failure. This failure, however, was our fault, and we learned an important lesson. This incident also highlighted the need for the Chaos Gorilla, which we successfully ran just a month later, intentionally taking out an entire zone's worth of servers to see what would happen (everything went smoothly). We ran another test of the Chaos Gorilla a few months later and learned even more about what were are doing right and where we could do better.

A few months later, there was another zone outage, this time due to the Elastic Block Store. Although we generally don't use EBS, many of our instances use EBS root volumes. As such, we had to abandon an availability zone. Luckily for us, our previous run of Chaos Gorilla gave us not only the confidence to make the call to abandon a zone, but also the tools to make it quick and relatively painless.

Looking back, there are plenty of other things we could have done to make reddit more resilient to failure, many of which I have learned through ad hoc trial and error, as well as from working at Netflix. Unfortunately, I didn't have a book like this one to guide me. This book outlines in excellent detail exactly how to build resilient systems in the cloud. From the crash course in systems to the detailed instructions on specific technologies, this book includes many of the very same things we stumbled upon as we flailed wildly, discovering solutions to problems. If I had had this book when I was first starting on AWS, I would have saved myself a lot of time and headache, and hopefully you will benefit from its knowledge after reading it.

This book also teaches a very important lesson: to embrace and expect failure, and if you do, you will be much better off.

—Jeremy Edberg, Information Cowboy, December 2012

Preface

Thank you (again) for picking up one of our books! If you have read Programming Amazon EC2 (*http://oreil.ly/Amazon_EC2*), you probably have some expectations about this book.

The idea behind this book came from Mike Loukides, one of our editors. He was fascinated with the idea of resilience and reliability in engineering. At the same time, Amazon Web Services (AWS) had been growing and growing.

As is the case for other systems, AWS does not go without service interruptions. The underlying architecture and available services are designed to help you deal with this. But as outages have shown, this is difficult, especially when you are powering the majority of the popular web services.

So how do we help people prepare? We already have a good book on the basics of engineering on AWS. But it deals with relatively simple applications, solely comprised of AWS's infrastructural components. What we wanted to show is how to build service components yourself and make them resilient and reliable.

The heart of this book is a collection of services we run in our infrastructures. We'll show things like Postgres and Redis, but also elasticsearch and MongoDB. But before we talk about these, we will introduce AWS and our approach to Resilience and Reliability.

We want to help you weather the next (AWS) outage!

Audience

If Amazon Web Services is new to you, we encourage you to pick up a copy of *Programming Amazon EC2*. Familiarize yourself with the many services AWS offers. It certainly helps to have worked (or played) with many of them.

Even though many of our components are nothing more than a collection of scripts (bash, Python, Ruby, PHP) don't be fooled. The lack of a development environment does not make it easier to engineer your way out of many problems.

Therefore, we feel this book is probably well-suited for software engineers. We use this term inclusively—not every programmer is a software engineer, and many system administrators are software engineers. But you at least need some experience building complex systems. It helps to have seen more than one programming language. And it certainly helps to have been responsible for operations.

Conventions Used in This Book

The following typographical conventions are used in this book:

Italic
> Indicates new terms, URLs, email addresses, filenames, and file extensions.

`Constant width`
> Used for program listings, as well as within paragraphs to refer to program elements such as variable or function names, databases, data types, environment variables, statements, and keywords.

`Constant width bold`
> Shows commands or other text that should be typed literally by the user.

`Constant width italic`
> Shows text that should be replaced with user-supplied values or by values determined by context.

> This icon signifies a tip, suggestion, or general note.

> This icon indicates a warning or caution.

Using Code Examples

This book is here to help you get your job done. In general, if this book includes code examples, you may use the code in this book in your programs and documentation. You do not need to contact us for permission unless you're reproducing a significant portion of the code. For example, writing a program that uses several chunks of code from this book does not require permission. Selling or distributing a CD-ROM of examples from O'Reilly books does require permission. Answering a question by citing this book and quoting example code does not require permission. Incorporating a significant amount of example code from this book into your product's documentation does require permission.

We appreciate, but do not require, attribution. An attribution usually includes the title, author, publisher, and ISBN. For example: "Resilience and Reliability on AWS (O'Reilly). Copyright 2013 9apps B.V., 978-1-449-33919-7."

If you feel your use of code examples falls outside fair use or the permission given above, feel free to contact us at *permissions@oreilly.com*.

Safari® Books Online

 *Safari Books Online* is an on-demand digital library that delivers expert content in both book and video form from the world's leading authors in technology and business.

Technology professionals, software developers, web designers, and business and creative professionals use Safari Books Online as their primary resource for research, problem solving, learning, and certification training.

Safari Books Online offers a range of product mixes and pricing programs for organizations, government agencies, and individuals. Subscribers have access to thousands of books, training videos, and prepublication manuscripts in one fully searchable database from publishers like O'Reilly Media, Prentice Hall Professional, Addison-Wesley Professional, Microsoft Press, Sams, Que, Peachpit Press, Focal Press, Cisco Press, John Wiley & Sons, Syngress, Morgan Kaufmann, IBM Redbooks, Packt, Adobe Press, FT Press, Apress, Manning, New Riders, McGraw-Hill, Jones & Bartlett, Course Technology, and dozens more. For more information about Safari Books Online, please visit us online.

How to Contact Us

Please address comments and questions concerning this book to the publisher:

O'Reilly Media, Inc.
1005 Gravenstein Highway North

Sebastopol, CA 95472
800-998-9938 (in the United States or Canada)
707-829-0515 (international or local)
707-829-0104 (fax)

We have a web page for this book, where we list errata, examples, and any additional information. You can access this page at *http://oreil.ly/Resilience_Reliability_AWS*.

To comment or ask technical questions about this book, send email to *bookques tions@oreilly.com*.

For more information about our books, courses, conferences, and news, see our website at *http://www.oreilly.com*.

Find us on Facebook: *http://facebook.com/oreilly*

Follow us on Twitter: *http://twitter.com/oreillymedia*

Watch us on YouTube: *http://www.youtube.com/oreillymedia*

Acknowledgments

There are many people we would like to thank for making this book into what it is now. But first of all, it would never have been possible without our parents, Franny Geurtsen, Jos Geurtsen, Aurora Gómez, Hans van Vliet, Marry van Vliet, and Ricardo Paganelli.

The work in this book is not ours alone. Our list will probably not be complete, and we apologize in advance if we forgot you, but we could not have written this book without the people from Publitas (Ali, Khalil, Guillermo, Dieudon, Dax, Felix), Qelp (Justin, Pascal, Martijn, Bas, Jasper), Olery (Wilco, Wijnand, Kim, Peter), Buzzer (Pim), Fashiolista (Thierry, Tomasso, Mike, Joost), Usabilla (Marc, Gijs, Paul), inSided (Wouter, Jochem, Maik), Poikos (Elleanor, David), Directness (Roy, Alessio, Adam), Marvia (Jons, Arnoud, Edwin, Tom), and Videodock (Bauke, Nick).

Of course, you need a fresh pair of eyes going over every detail and meticulously trying out examples to find errors. Our technical reviewers, Dave Ward and Mitch Garnaat, did just that.

And finally, there is the wonderful and extremely professional team at O'Reilly. Without Mike, Meghan, and all the others there wouldn't even have been a book. Thank you!

## CHAPTER 1

Introduction

The Cloud is new, in whatever guise it chooses to show itself. All the clouds we know today are relatively young. But more importantly, they introduce a new paradigm.

The cloud we talk about in this book is Amazon Web Services (or AWS). AWS is infrastructure as a service (IaaS), but it does not respect these cloud qualifications very much. You can find different AWS services in other types of cloud like PaaS (platform as a service) or even SaaS (software as a service).

In our *Programming Amazon EC2* book, we introduced Amazon AWS. We tried to help people get from one side of the chasm to the other. From the traditional viewpoint of administration, this is nearly impossible to do. From the perspective of the developer, it is just as problematic, but reintroducing the discipline of software engineering makes it easier.

Programming Amazon EC2 covers AWS in its full breadth. If you want to know how to design your app, build your infrastructure, and run your AWS-based operations, that book will certainly get you up to speed. What it doesn't do, however, is explicitly deal with Resilience and Reliability.

That is what this book aims to do. For us, Resilience means the ability to recover. And Reliable means that the recovery is not luck but rather something you can really trust.

First, we will explain how we look at infrastructures and infrastructural components. It is remarkably similar to building in the physical world. Perhaps the main difference is flexibility, but that might be just as much a curse as a blessing. It will require you to take a holistic view of your application and its use of resources.

We will also do an overview of AWS, but beware that this is extremely concise. However, if you are pressed for time, it will familiarize you with the basic concepts. If you need more in-depth knowledge of AWS, there are other books…

A "top 10" of something is always very popular. Memorize them and you can hold your own in any conversation. Our Top 10 Survival Tips are our best practices. You can overlay them on your current (cloud) infrastructure, and see where the holes are.

The rest of the book is devoted to examples and stories of how we approach and engineer our solutions using:

- elasticsearch
- Postgres
- MongoDB
- Redis
- Logstash
- Global Delivery

These examples are meant to illustrate certain concepts. But, most importantly, we hope they inspire you to build your own solutions.

## CHAPTER 2

The Road to Resilience and Reliability

If you build and/or operate an important application, it doesn't matter if it is large or small. The thing you care about is that it works. Under ideal circumstances, this is not very difficult. But those kinds of circumstances are a dream. In every environment there is failure. The question is how to deal with it.

This problem is not new. The traditional point of resolution used to be the IT department. Due to several factors, that is changing. Operations is more and more part of software, and building infrastructures is software engineering.

To introduce the book, we'll first discuss our strategy. If infrastructure is software, we can apply our software engineering principles.

Once Upon a Time, There Was a Mason

One of the most important problems that software engineers have to solve is how to reuse work (code). Reusing code means you reduce the size of the code base, and as a consequence, there is less work in development and testing. Maintenance is also much more effective; multiple projects can benefit from improvements in one piece of code.

There are many solutions to this problem of how to reuse code. First, with structured programming, there were methods (functions/procedures). Later on, object-oriented programming introduced even more tools to handle this challenge, with objects, classes, and inheritance, for example.

There are also domain-specific tools and environments, often called frameworks. These frameworks offer a structure (think of the Model View Controller design pattern for user interfaces) and building blocks (such as classes to interface with a database).

At this stage we are basically like masons. We have our tools and materials and our body of knowledge on how to use them. With this, we can build the most amazing (infra)structures, which happen to be *resilient* and *reliable* (most of the time). But, as Wikipedia states, we need something else as well:

> *Masonry* is generally a highly durable form of construction. However, the materials used, the quality of the mortar and workmanship, and the pattern in which the units are assembled can significantly affect the durability of the overall masonry construction.

In this analogy we choose IaaS (Infrastructure as a Service) as our framework. The basic building blocks for IaaS are compute (servers) and storage (not only in the form of disks). The defining features of IaaS are on-demand and pay-as-you-go. Many IaaS platforms (or providers) offer one or more layers of service on top of this. Most of the time these are built with the basic building blocks.

Our IaaS is Amazon Web Services. AWS comes with Elastic Compute Cloud (EC2) and Elastic Block Store (EBS), for computing and storage, respectively. AWS also provides Simple Storage Service (S3) as a virtually infinite storage web service which does not follow the *disk paradigm*. AWS offers more sophisticated services, like Relational Database Service (RDS) providing turnkey Oracle/MySQL/SQLServer, and ElastiCache for memcached, a popular caching technology. We will extend the framework with our own solutions.

Now, we have everything to build those amazing (infra)structures, but, unlike in the physical world, we can construct and tear down our cathedrals in minutes. And this enables us to work in different ways than a mason. You can host 26,000 people on Sunday, but literally scale down to a church fitting a more modest group of people during the week.

Rip. Mix. Burn.

With the flexibility given by being able to construct and destroy components whenever we want, we gain enormous freedom. We can literally play with infrastructures whose underlying hardware is worth tens or hundreds of thousands of dollars—not for free, of course, but relatively affordably.

The multitude of freely available—often open source—technologies gives us lots of building blocks ("rip"). Some examples we will use are MongoDB and Redis. These building blocks can be turned into application infrastructures with the resources of AWS ("mix"). We can keep these infrastructures while we need them, and just discard them when we don't. And we can easily reproduce and recreate the infrastructure or some of its components again ("burn"), for example, in case of failures, or for creating pipelines in development, testing, staging, and production environments.

Cradle to Cradle

The dynamic nature of our application infrastructures has another interesting consequence. The lifecycle of individual components has changed. Before, we would be measuring the uptime of a server, trying to get it to live as long as possible. Now, we strive to renew individual components as often as possible; decomposing has become just as important as constructing.

Systems have to stay healthy. They have to do their fair share of work. If they don't, we have to intervene, preferably in an automated way. We might have to change parts, like replacing an EC2 instance for a bigger one if computing power is not enough. Sometimes replacing is enough to get our health back.

And, in the end, we return the unused resources for future use.

This way of working in the material world is called Cradle to Cradle. The benefits are not only environmental. Organizations restructuring their way of doing business according to this methodology will:

- Use fewer resources (on-demand, pay-as-you-go)
- Use cheaper resources (off-hours at lower rates)

Because of this it is often reported that these organizations have a lower financial cost of systems.

In Short

In this chapter we introduced our general approach to building resilient and reliable applications. This approach might sound a bit abstract at this point, but we will be using this philosophy the rest of the book. It can be compared with the work of a mason, where you have a set of building blocks, and you put them together to build a structure. In our case we can also easily decompose, destroy, and rebuild our components and infrastructures, by switching AWS resources on and off.

## CHAPTER 3

Crash Course in AWS

Amazon AWS at the time of writing offers 33 services. We will not talk about all of them, mostly because they are not relevant to the theme of this book.

In this chapter we will highlight the core AWS services we use to build the components we talked about in the previous chapter. For those of you who have read *Programming Amazon EC2*, you can see this as a refresher. There we used nearly two hundred pages to describe these services and how to use them. Here we will condense it to one-tenth of that, including some new AWS services released recently.

If you are familiar with AWS services, you can skip this chapter, or just read those sections about the services you don't know about. This chapter details all AWS services used in the remainder of the book (Figure 3-1). You can also use this chapter as a reference and come back to it later as necessary.

For the rest of the book, prior knowledge and experience with AWS is not necessary, but a good understanding of the services in this and the next chapter is instrumental.

In addition to being shown in the AWS Management Console, AWS services are exposed programmatically via a set of well defined APIs, implemented as web services. These can be accessed via command line tools or any of the different libraries or toolkits in the different programming languages (Java, PHP, Ruby, etc.). From now on, we will use the terms "API" or "APIs" to refer to the different ways AWS can be accessed; see the code page (*http://aws.amazon.com/code*) on the AWS site.

Regions and Availability Zones

EC2 and S3 (and a number of other services, see Figure 3-1) are organized in *regions*. All regions provide more or less the same services, and everything we talk about in this chapter applies to all the available AWS regions.

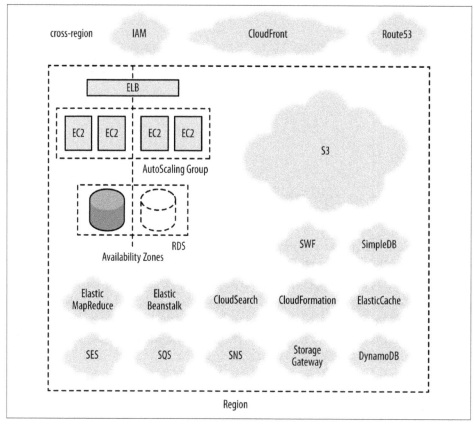

Figure 3-1. Overview of some of AWS services

A region is comprised of two or more *availability zones* (Figure 3-2), each zone consisting of one or more distinct data centers. Availability zones are designed to shield our infrastructures from physical harm, like thunderstorms or hurricanes, for example. If one data center is damaged, you should be able to use another one by switching to another availability zone. Availability zones are, therefore, important in getting your apps resilient and reliable.

Route 53: Domain Name System Service

If you register a domain, you often get the Domain Name System service for free. Your registrar will give you access to a web application where you can manage your records. This part of your infrastructure is often overlooked. But it is a notoriously weak spot; if it fails, no one will be able to reach your site. And it is often outside of your control.

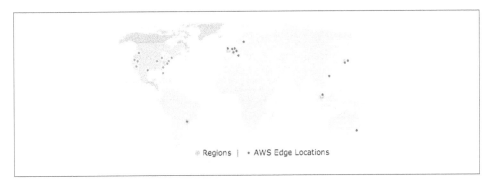

Figure 3-2. AWS regions and edge locations

There were three or four high quality, commercial DNS services before AWS introduced Route 53. The features of all of these DNS services are more or less similar, but the prices can vary enormously. Route 53 changed this market. It offered basic features for a fraction of the price of competing offerings.

But Route 53 is different in its approach. DNS is viewed as a dynamic part of its software, which you can utilize for things like failover or application provisioning. Services like RDS and ElastiCache rely heavily on Route 53 (behind the scenes, for the most part).

Just as AWS does, we often rely on the programmatic nature of Route 53. As you will see in later chapters we will implement failover strategies with relative ease.

Not all software is ready for the dynamic nature of DNS. The assumption often is that DNS records hardly change. These systems adopt an aggressive caching mechanism (just never resolve domain names again for the duration of the execution) that breaks when underlying IP addresses change.

Route 53 is a very important tool at our disposal!

IAM (Identity and Access Management)

IAM is exactly what it says it is. It lets you manage identities that can be allowed (or denied) access to AWS resources. Access is granted on services (API actions) or resources (things like S3 buckets or EC2 instances). Access can be organized by *users* and *groups*. Both users and groups have permissions assigned to them by way of *policies*. The user's *credentials* are used to authenticate with the AWS web services. A user can belong to zero or more groups.

You can use IAM to give access to people. And you can use it to give access to particular components. For example, an elasticsearch EC2 instance (more about this in Chapter 5) only needs restricted read access on the EC2 API to "discover" the cluster, and it needs restricted read/write access on S3 on a particular *bucket* (a sort of folder) for making backups.

Access is granted in *policies*. For example, the following policy allows access to all EC2 API operations starting with Describe, on all resources (or globally), some kind of read-only policy for EC2:

```
{
  "Statement": [
    {
      "Effect": "Allow",
      "Action": "EC2:Describe*",
      "Resource": "*"
    }
  ]
}
```

 IAM is VERY important

This service is very, very important. It not only protects you from serious exposure in case of security breaches; it also protects you from inadvertent mistakes or bugs. If you only have privileges to work on one particular S3 bucket, you can do no harm to the rest.

IAM has many interesting features, but two deserve to be mentioned explicitly. Multi Factor Authentication (MFA) adds a second authentication step to particular operations. Just assuming a particular identity is not enough; you are prompted for a dynamic security code generated by a physical or virtual device that you own, before you can proceed.

The second feature that needs to be mentioned explicitly is that you can add a *role* to an EC2 instance. The role's policies will then determine all the permissions available from that instance. This means that you no longer need to do a lot of work rotating (replacing) access credentials, something that is a tedious-to-implement security best practice.

The Basics: EC2, RDS, ElastiCache, S3, CloudFront, SES, and CloudWatch

The basic services of any IaaS (Infrastructure as a Service) are **compute** and **storage**. AWS offers compute as EC2 (Elastic Compute Cloud) and storage as S3 (Simple Storage Service). These two services are the absolute core of everything that happens on Amazon AWS.

RDS (Relational Database Service) is "database as a service," hiding many of the difficulties of databases behind a service layer. This has been built with EC2 and S3.

CloudFront is the CDN (Content Distribution Network) AWS offers. It helps you distribute static, dynamic, and streaming content to many places in the world.

Simple Email Service (SES) helps you send mails. You can use it for very large batches. We just always use it, because it is reliable and has a very high deliverability (spam is not solved only by Outlook or Gmail).

We grouped the services like this because these are the basic services for a web application: we have computing, storage, relational database services, content delivery, and email sending. So, bear with us, here we go…

CloudWatch

CloudWatch is AWS's own monitoring solution. All AWS services come with metrics on resource utilization. An EC2 instance has metrics for CPU utilization, network, and IO. Next to those metrics, an RDS instance also creates metrics on memory and disk usage.

CloudWatch has its own tab in the console, and from there you can browse metrics and look at measurements over periods of up to two weeks. You can look at multiple metrics at the same time, comparing patterns of utilization.

You can also add your own custom metrics. For example, if you build your own managed solution for MongoDB, you can add custom metrics for all sorts of operational parameters, as we will see in Chapter 7. Figure 3-3 shows a chart of the "resident memory" metric in a MongoDB replica set.

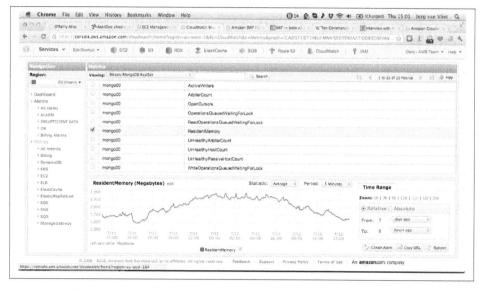

Figure 3-3. Showing some MongoDB-specific metrics using CloudWatch

EC2 (et al.)

To understand EC2 (Figure 3-4) you need to be familiar with a number of concepts:

- Instance
- Image (Amazon Machine Image, AMI)
- Volume and Snapshot (EBS and S3)
- Security Group
- Elastic IP

There are other concepts we will not discuss here, like Virtual Private Cloud (VPC), which has some features (such as multiple IP addresses and flexible networking) that can help you make your application more resilient and reliable. But some of these concepts can be implemented with other AWS services like IAM or Route 53.

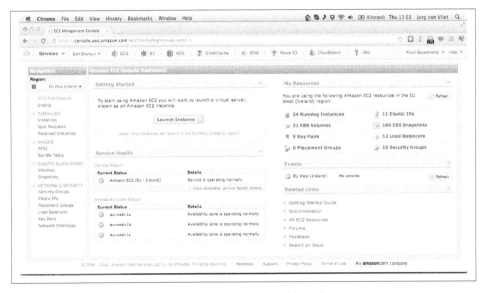

Figure 3-4. Screenshot from AWS Console, EC2 Dashboard

Instance

An *instance* is a server, nothing more and nothing less. Instances are launched from an *image* (an AMI) into an availability zone. There are S3-backed instances, a kind of ephemeral storage in which the root device is part of the instance itself. (Instances launched from an S3-backed AMI cannot be stopped and started; they can only be restarted or terminated.) EBS-backed instances, which are more the norm now, provide block level storage volumes that persist independently of the instance (that is, the root/ boot disk is on a separate EBS volume, allowing the instance to be stopped and started). See "Volume and snapshot (EBS and S3)" (page 15).

> ### Dependencies
>
> EBS still has a dependency on S3 (when a new volume is created from an existing S3 snapshot). Even though this dependency is extremely reliable, it might not be a good idea to increase dependencies.

Instances come in *types* (sizes). Types used to be restricted to either 32-bit or 64-bit operating systems, but since early 2012 all instance types are capable of running 64-bit. We work mainly with Ubuntu, and we mostly run 64-bit now. There are the following instance types (*http://aws.amazon.com/ec2/instance-types/*):

Small Instance (m1.small) – default
    1.7 GB memory, 1 EC2 Compute Unit

Medium Instance (m1.medium)
    3.75 GB memory, 2 EC2 Compute Unit

Large Instance (m1.large)
    7.5 GB memory, 4 EC2 Compute Units

Extra Large Instance (m1.xlarge)
    15 GB memory, 8 EC2 Compute Units

Micro Instance (t1.micro)
    613 MB memory, Up to 2 EC2 Compute Units (for short periodic bursts)

High-Memory Extra Large Instance (m2.xlarge)
    17.1 GB of memory, 6.5 EC2 Compute Units

High-Memory Double Extra Large Instance (m2.2xlarge)
    34.2 GB of memory, 13 EC2 Compute Units

High-Memory Quadruple Extra Large Instance (m2.4xlarge)
    68.4 GB of memory, 26 EC2 Compute Units

High-CPU Medium Instance (c1.medium)
    1.7 GB of memory, 5 EC2 Compute Units

High-CPU Extra Large Instance (c1.xlarge)
    7 GB of memory, 20 EC2 Compute Units

The *micro* instance is "fair use." You can burst CPU for short periods of time, but when you misbehave and use too much, your CPU capacity is capped for a certain amount of time.

For higher requirements, such as high performance computing, there are also *cluster* type instances, with increased CPU and network performance, including one with graphics processing units. Recently Amazon also released *high I/O* instances, which give very high storage performance by using SSD (Solid State Drives) devices.

At launch, an instance can be given *user data*. User data is exposed on the instance through a locally accessible web service. In the bash Unix shell, we can get the user data as follows (in this case json). The output is an example from the Mongo setup we will explain in Chapter 7, so don't worry about it for now:

```
$ curl --silent http://169.254.169.254/latest/user-data/ | python -mjson.tool
{
    "name"       :    "mongodb",
    "size"       :    100,
    "role"       :    "active"
}
```

Almost all information about the instance is exposed through this interface. You can learn the private IP address, the public hostname, etc.:

```
$ curl --silent http://169.254.169.254/latest/meta-data/public-hostname
ec2-46-137-11-123.eu-west-1.compute.amazonaws.com
```

Image (AMI, Amazon Machine Image)

An AMI is a bit like a boot CD. You launch an instance from an AMI. You have 32-bit AMIs and 64-bit AMIs. Anything that runs on the XEN Hypervisor (*http://www.xen.org*) can run on Amazon AWS and thus be turned into an AMI.

There are ways to make AMIs from scratch. These days that is not necessary unless you are Microsoft, Ubuntu, or you want something extremely special. We could also launch an Ubuntu AMI provided by Canonical, change the instance, and make our own AMI from that.

AMIs are cumbersome to work with, but they are the most important raw ingredient of your application infrastructures. AMIs just need to work. And they need to work reliably, always giving the same result. There is no simulator for working with AMIs, except EC2 itself. (EBS-backed AMIs are so much easier to work with that we almost forgot S3-backed AMIs still exist.)

If you use AMIs from third parties, make sure to verify their origin (which is now easier to do than before.)

Volume and snapshot (EBS and S3)

EBS (Elastic Block Store) is one of the of the more interesting inventions of AWS. It has been introduced to persist local storage, because S3 (Simple Storage Service) was not enough to work with.

Basically EBS offers disks, or *volumes,* between 1 GB and 1 TB in size. A volume resides in an availability zone, and can be attached to one (and only one) instance. An EBS volume can have a point-in-time snapshot taken, from which the volume can be restored. Snapshots are regional, but not bound to an availability zone.

If you need disks (local storage) that are persistent (you have to make your own backups) you use EBS.

EBS is a new technology. As such, it has seen its fair share of difficulties. But it is very interesting and extremely versatile. See the coming chapters (the chapter on Postgres in particular) for how we capitalize on the opportunities EBS gives.

Security group

Instances are part of one or more *security groups*. With these security groups, you can shield off instances from the outside world. You can expose them on only certain ports or port ranges, or for certain IP masks, like you would do with a firewall. Also you can restrict access to instances which are inside specific security groups.

Security groups give you a lot of flexibility to selectively expose your assets.

VPC

VPC (Virtual Private Cloud) offers much more functionality as part of the Security Groups. For example, it is not possible to restrict incoming connections in *normal* security groups. With VPC you can control both incoming and outgoing connections.

Elastic IP

Instances are automatically assigned a public IP address. This address changes with every instance launch. If you have to identify a particular part of your application through an instance and therefore use an address that doesn't change, you can use an *elastic IP* (EIP). You can associate and dissociate them from instances, manually in the console or through the API.

Route 53 makes elastic IPs almost obsolete. But many software packages do not yet gracefully handle DNS changes. If this is the case, using an elastic IP might help you.

RDS

Amazon's RDS (Relational Database Service) now comes in three different flavors: MySQL, Oracle, and Microsoft SQLServer. You can basically run one of these databases, production ready, commercial grade. You can scale up and down in minutes. You can grow storage without service interruption. And you can restore your data up to 31 days back.

The maximum storage capacity is 1 TB. Important metrics are exposed through Cloud-Watch. In Figure 3-5 you can see, for example, the CPU utilization of an instance. This service will be explained more in detail later.

The only thing RDS doesn't do for you is optimize your schema!

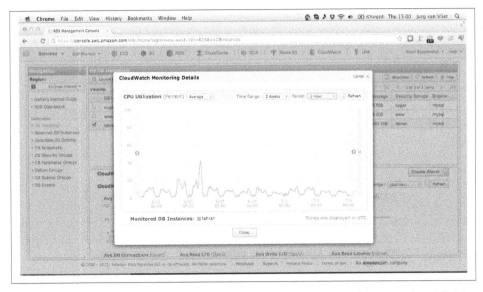

Figure 3-5. Screenshot from the AWS Console, showing CPU utilization of an RDS instance

ElastiCache

This is like RDS for *memcached*, an object caching protocol often used to relieve the database and/or speed up sites and apps. This technology is not very difficult to run, but it does require close monitoring. Before ElastiCache, we always ran it by hand, replacing instances when they died.

ElastiCache adds the ability to easily grow or shrink a memcached cluster. Unfortunately you can't easily change the type of the instances used. But more importantly, ElastiCache manages failure. If a node fails to operate, it will replace it.

As with other services, it exposes a number of operational metrics through CloudWatch. These can be used for capacity planning, or to understand other parts of your system's behavior.

S3/CloudFront

S3 stands for *Simple Storage Service*. This is probably the most revolutionary service AWS offers at this moment. S3 allows you to store an unlimited amount of data. If you do not delete your objects yourself, it is almost impossible for them to be corrupt or lost entirely. S3 has 99.999999999% durability.

You can create buckets in any of the regions. And you can store an unlimited amount of objects per bucket, with a size between 1 byte to 5 TB.

S3 is reliable storage exposed through a web service. For many things this is fast enough, but not for static assets of websites or mobile applications. For these assets, AWS introduced *CloudFront*, a CDN (Content Distribution Network).

CloudFront can expose an S3 bucket, or it can be used with what AWS calls a *custom origin* (another site). On top of S3, CloudFront distributes the objects to edge locations all over the world, so latency is reduced considerably. Apart from getting them closer to the users, it offloads some of the heavy lifting your application or web servers used to do.

SES

Sending mails in a way that they actually arrive is getting more and more difficult. On AWS you can have your elastic IP whitelisted automatically. But it still requires operating an MTA (Mail Transfer Agent) like Postfix. But with *Amazon SES* (Simple Email System) this has all become much easier.

After signing up for the service you have to practice a bit in the sandbox before you can request production access. It might take a while before you earn the right to send a significant volume. But if you use SES from the start, you have no problems when your service takes off.

Growing Up: ELB, Auto Scaling

Elasticity is still the promise of "The Cloud." If the traffic increases, you get yourself more capacity, only to release it when you don't need it anymore. The game is to increase utilization, often measured in terms of the CPU utilization. The other way of seeing it is to decrease waste, and be more efficient.

AWS has two important services to help us with this. The first is ELB, or Elastic Load Balancer. The second is Auto Scaling.

ELB (Elastic Load Balancer)

An ELB sits in front of a group of instances. You can reach an ELB through a hostname. Or, with Route 53, you can have your records resolve directly to the IP addresses of the ELB.

An ELB can distribute any kind of TCP traffic. It also distributes HTTP and HTTPS. The ELB will *terminate* HTTPS and talk plain HTTP to the instances. This is convenient, and reduces the load on the instances behind.

Traffic is evenly distributed across one or more availability zones, which you configure in the ELB. Remember that every EC2 instance runs in a particular availability zone. Within an availability zone, the ELB distributes the traffic evenly over the instances. It has no sophisticated (or complicated) routing policies. Instances are either healthy, determined with a configurable health check, or not. A health check could be something like pinging /status.html on HTTP every half a minute, and a response status 200 would mean the instance is healthy.

ELBs are a good alternative for elastic IPs. ELBs cost some money in contrast to elastic IPs (which are free while they are associated to an instance), but ELBs increase security and reduce the complexity of the infrastructure. You can use an auto scaling group (see below) to automatically register and unregister the instance, instead of managing elastic IP attachments yourself.

ELBs are versatile and the features are fine, but they are still a bit immature and the promise of surviving availability zone problems are not always met. It's not always the case that when one availability zone fails, the ELB keeps running normally on the other availability zones. We choose to work with AWS to improve this technology, instead of building (and maintaining) something ourselves.

Auto Scaling

If you want an elastic group of instances that resizes based on demand, you want Auto Scaling. This service helps you coordinate these groups of instances.

Auto Scaling launches and terminates instances based on CloudWatch metrics. For example, you can use the average CPU utilization (or any of the other instance metrics available) of the instances in the group itself. You could configure your group so that every time the average CPU utilization of your group is over 60% for a period of 5 minutes, it will launch two new instances. If it goes below 10%, it will terminate two instances. You can make sure the group is never empty by setting the minimum size to two.

You can resize the group based on any CloudWatch metric available. When using SQS (see below) for a job queue, you can grow and shrink the group's capacity based on the number of items in that queue. And you can also use CloudWatch custom metrics. For example, you could create a custom metric for the number of connections to NGiNX or Apache, and use that to determine the desired capacity.

Auto Scaling ties in nicely with ELBs, as they can register and unregister instances automatically. At this point, this mechanism is still rather blunt. Instances are first removed and terminated before a new one is launched and has the chance to become "in service."

Decoupling: SQS, SimpleDB & DynamoDB, SNS, SWF

The services we have discussed so far are great for helping you build a good web application. But when you reach a certain scale, you will require something else.

If your app starts to get so big that your individual components can't handle it any more, there is only one solution left: to break your app into multiple smaller apps. This method is called *decoupling*.

Decoupling is very different from sharding. Sharding is horizontal partitioning across instances and it can help you in certain circumstances, but is extremely difficult to do well. If you feel the need for sharding, look around. With different components (DynamoDB, Cassandra, elasticsearch, etc.) and decoupling, you are probably better off not sharding.

Amazon travelled down this path before. The first service to see the light was SQS, Simple Queue Service. Later other services followed like SimpleDB and SNS (Simple Notification Service). And only recently (early 2012) they introduced SWF, Simple Workflow Service.

These services are like the glue of your decoupled system: they bind the individual apps or components together. They are designed to be very reliable and scalable, for which they had to make some tradeoffs. But at scale you have different problems to worry about.

If you consider growing *beyond* the relational database model (either in scale or in features) DynamoDB is a very interesting alternative. You can provision your DynamoDB database to be able to handle insane amounts of transactions. It does require some administration, but completely negligible compared to building and operating your own Cassandra cluster or MongoDB Replica Set (See Chapter 7).

SQS (Simple Queue Service)

In the SQS Developer Guide, you can read that "Amazon SQS is a distributed queue system that enables web service applications to quickly and reliably queue messages that one component in the application generates to be consumed by another component. A queue is a temporary repository for messages that are awaiting processing" (Figure 3-6).

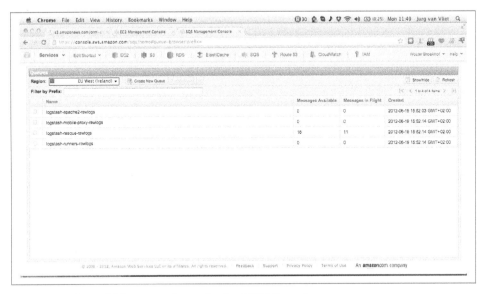

Figure 3-6. Some SQS queues shown in the AWS Console

And that's basically all it is. You can have many writers hitting a queue at the same time. SQS does its best to preserve order, but the distributed nature makes it impossible to guarantee this. If you really need to preserve order, you can add your own identifier as part of the queued messages, but approximate order is probably enough to work with in most cases. A trade-off like this is necessary in massively scalable services like SQS. This is not very different from *eventual consistency*, as is the case in S3 and in SimpleDB.

In addition to many writers hitting a queue at the same time, you can also have many readers, and SQS guarantees each message is delivered at least once (more than once if the receiving reader doesn't delete it from the queue). Reading a message is atomic; locks are used to keep multiple readers from processing the same message. Because you can't assume a message will be processed successfully and deleted, SQS first sets it to *invisible*. This invisibility has an expiration, called *visibility timeout*, that defaults to thirty seconds. After processing the message, it must be deleted explicitly (if successful, of course). If it's not deleted and the timeout expires, the message shows up in the queue again. If 30 seconds is not enough, the timeout can be configured in the queue or per message, although the recommended way is to use different queues for different visibility timeouts.

You can have as many queues as you want, but leaving them inactive is a violation of intended use. We couldn't figure out what the penalties are, but the principle of cloud computing is to minimize waste. Message size is variable, and the maximum is 64 KB. If you need to work with larger objects, the obvious place to store them is S3.

One last important thing to remember is that messages are not retained indefinitely. Messages will be deleted after four days by default, but you can have your queue retain them for a maximum of two weeks.

SimpleDB

AWS says that SimpleDB is "a highly available, scalable, and flexible nonrelational data store that offloads the work of database administration." There you have it! In other words, you can store an extreme amount of structured information without worrying about security, data loss, and query performance. And you pay only for what you use.

SimpleDB is not a relational database, but to explain what it is, we will compare it to a relational database since that's what we know best. SimpleDB is not a database server, so therefore there is no such thing in SimpleDB as a database. In SimpleDB, you create *domains* to store related *items*. Items are collections of *attributes*, or key-value pairs. The attributes can have multiple values. An item can have 256 attributes and a domain can have one billion attributes; together, this may take up to 10 GB of storage.

You can compare a domain to a table, and an item to a record in that table. A traditional relational database imposes the structure by defining a schema. A SimpleDB domain does not require items to be all of the same structure. It doesn't make sense to have all totally different items in one domain, but you can change the attributes you use over time. As a consequence, you can't define indexes, but they are implicit: every attribute is indexed automatically for you.

Domains are distinct—they are on their own. Joins, which are the most powerful feature in relational databases, are not possible. You cannot combine the information in two domains with one single query. Joins were introduced to reconstruct normalized data, where normalizing data means ripping it apart to avoid duplication.

Because of the lack of joins, there are two different approaches to handling relations. You can either introduce duplication (for instance, by storing employees in the employer domain and vice versa), or you can use multiple queries and combine the data at the application level. If you have data duplication and if several applications write to your SimpleDB domains, each of them will have to be aware of this when you make changes or add items to maintain consistency. In the second case, each application that reads your data will need to aggregate information from different domains.

There is one other aspect of SimpleDB that is important to understand. If you add or update an item, it does not have to be immediately available. SimpleDB reserves the right to take some time to process the operations you fire at it. This is what is called *eventual consistency*, and for many kinds of information getting a slightly earlier version of that information is not a huge problem.

But in some cases, you need the latest, most up-to-date information, and for these cases, consistency can be enforced. Think of an online auction website like eBay, where people bid for different items. At the moment a purchase is made, it's important that the correct (latest) price is read from the database. To address those situations, SimpleDB introduced two new features in early 2010: *consistent read* and *conditional put/delete*. A consistent read guarantees to return values that reflect all previously successful writes. Conditional put/delete guarantees that a certain operation is performed only when one of the attributes exists or has a particular value. With this, you can implement a counter, for example, or implement locking/concurrency.

We have to stress that SimpleDB is a service, and as such, it solves a number of problems for you. Indexing is one we already mentioned. High availability, performance, and infinite scalability are other benefits. You don't have to worry about replicating your data to protect it against hardware failures, and you don't have to think of what hardware you are using if you have more load, or how to handle peaks. Also, the software upgrades are taken care of for you.

But even though SimpleDB makes sure your data is safe and highly available by seamlessly replicating it in several data centers, Amazon itself doesn't provide a way to manually make backups. So if you want to protect your data against your own mistakes and be able to revert back to previous versions, you will have to resort to third-party solutions that can back up SimpleDB data, for example by using S3.

SNS (Simple Notification Service)

Both SQS and SimpleDB are kind of passive, or static. You can add things, and if you need something from it, you have to pull. This is OK for many services, but sometimes you need something more disruptive; you need to push instead of pull. This is what Amazon SNS gives us. You can push information to any component that is listening, and the messages are delivered right away.

SNS is not an easy service, but it is incredibly versatile. Luckily, we are all living in "the network society," so the essence of SNS should be familiar to most of us. It is basically the same concept as a mailing list or LinkedIn group—there is something you are interested in (a *topic*, in SNS-speak), and you show that interest by subscribing. Once the topic verifies that you exist by confirming the subscription, you become part of the group receiving messages on that topic.

SNS can be seen as an event system, but how does it work? First, you create topics. Topics are the conduits for sending (publishing) and receiving messages, or events. Anyone with an AWS account can subscribe to a topic, though that doesn't mean they will be automatically permitted to receive messages. And the topic owner can subscribe non-AWS users on their behalf. Every subscriber has to explicitly "opt in," though that term is usually related to mailing lists and spam; it is the logical consequence in an open system like the Web (you can see this as the equivalent of border control in a country).

The most interesting thing about SNS has to do with the subscriber, the recipient of the messages. A subscriber can configure an end point, specifying how and where the message will be delivered. Currently SNS supports three types of end points: HTTP/ HTTPS, email, and SQS; this is exactly the reason we feel it is more than a notification system. You can integrate an API using SNS, enabling totally different ways of execution.

SWF (Simple Workflow Service)

Simple Workflow Service helps you build and run complex process flows. It takes a workflow description and fires two tasks. Some tasks require a decision that affects the flow of the process; these are handled by a decider. Other, more mundane tasks, are handled by workers.

If your application requires some kind of workflow you usually start with a couple of cron jobs. If this starts to get out of hand, task queues and workers take over that role. This is a huge advantage, especially if you use a service like SQS.

But, if your process flows get more complex, the application starts to bloat. Information about current state and history starts to creep into your application. This is not desirable, to say the least, especially not at scale.

heystaq.com, one of our own applications, is about rating AWS infrastructures. Our core business is to say something knowledgable about an infrastructure, not manage hundreds of workflows generating thousands of individual tasks. For heystaq.com we could build a workflow for scanning the AWS infrastructure. We could scan instances, volumes, snapshots, ELBs, etc. Some of these tasks are related, like instances and volumes. Others can easily be run in parallel.

We also scan for CloudWatch alarms, and add those alarms if they are not present. We could create another SWF workflow for this. Now we have two, entirely unrelated sequences of activities that can be run in any combination. And, as a consequence, we can auto scale our system on demand relatively easily. (We'll show you how we do this in a later chapter.)

## CHAPTER 4

Top 10 Survival Tips

Outages are the norm, not the exception, and though they are rare, they are inevitable. This is something we all have to deal with.

Amazon AWS has been designed with failure in mind, and you can do a number of things to survive outages and other kinds of problems.

Make a Choice

At this point there are very few public cloud vendors that offer a comparable suite of services to Amazon AWS. This is only a matter time.

There are several *cloud management tools* that advertise multi-vendor (multi-cloud) as their core feature. They try to frighten you into purchasing their added complexity. The result is that you can't use the more sophisticated services of one cloud, because they are not supported on another.

The core reason to use a public cloud is to get rid of the burden to own and manage these types of infrastructures. You pay your cloud vendor to handle the responsibility of making sure there are facilities to properly handle failure. If they do not deliver, you move on.

Instead of wasting time supporting multiple clouds, we choose Amazon AWS. Because we make this choice, we can use all of their services if they make sense for us. We do not worry if they are supported on other clouds; we just use them because they save us time and money.

Embrace Change

Even though the cloud has dominated technology news for years, this is still uncharted territory. Existing systems reflect this and are not well prepared for the nature of this type of infrastructure platform.

Features that are considered old (tablespaces in Postgres) can be given new life with services like EBS from AWS. Existing automation tools feel awkward in dynamic environments built on top of AWS with things like images and snapshots.

Also the work changes. Infrastructure literally moves into software engineering. And we are not ready yet.

So be ready for change. Embrace it. You might have spent three months building a workflow tool only to learn about SWF. Embrace this, and refactor if you think it will improve your system. Look for these opportunities, and take full advantage of them.

Everything Will Break

Failure is something we have always known but never accepted. We have been buying system components with dual-anything, to prevent them from breaking. We have spent a lot of time trying to get rid of malfunction.

Well, the world is not perfect, and we will never be able to completely avoid malfunctions. Things will break; systems will fail.

You may lose a snapshot of your system, which may not be a big problem if you have more recent snapshots. But if you lose a snapshot from an image that you rely on for recovery you really do have to act on that.

You may lose a volume, too, which is not a problem if it is not used and you have a recent snapshot. But it is definitely a problem if you have data you didn't persist somewhere else. (It turns out that snapshotting rejuvenates your volumes.)

Life Expectancy of an EBS Volume

An EBS volume is cached. The cache contains the diffs since the last snapshot. Every diff is another item that can fail. Less diffs, less chance of failure.

You can lose instances. You can even lose entire Availability Zones. You know this, so you shouldn't act surprised when it happens. AWS has multiple Availability Zones, and you should use them. They have an almost unlimited supply of instances, so make sure you can replace your instances easily. And a snapshot doesn't cost very much, so make sure you take them often enough.

Know Your Enemy

For the sake of our top 10 tips, we'll consider AWS our enemy. They do not make many promises, and in fact they stress as many times as possible that things will break. Make sure everyone has a basic understanding of AWS-style cloud engineering. All your software developers need to understand about the different ways to persist data in AWS. Everyone needs to have a basic architectural understanding. They need to know about services like SQS and ELB. It is a good idea to share operational responsibility, as that is the fastest way to disseminate this information.

Netflix introduced a rather radical approach to this. Instead of failure scenarios, they introduced failure itself. Their Chaos Monkey (*https://github.com/Netflix/SimianArmy/wiki*) wreaks havoc continuously in their production infrastructure.

Know Yourself

A good understanding of AWS alone is not enough. You need to know yourself as well. Be sure to spend time building failure scenarios and testing them to see what happens. If you have practiced with these scenarios your teams will be trained, there will be fewer surprises, and even the surprises will be handled much better.

There is always something that can be improved upon in terms of Resilience and Reliability. Make it a priority for everyone to have a personal top 3!

Engineer for Today

If you build your stuff for the problems you have now, you will stay focused and do the right things. This doesn't mean that you can only solve small problems—it means that you can steer clear of doing unnecessary or expensive things that do not add value.

This is the main reason why we always try to use as many *off-the-shelf components*, preferably from AWS. Perhaps ELB is not perfect yet, but we choose to work on features, instead of operating multi-availability-zone load balancers.

Same goes for RDS. You can debate whether Postgres has better transaction support than MySQL. But with RDS we move on to working on application functionality, instead of building a highly available Postgres database that looks like RDS.

So, pick your targets and stay focused. Don't spend time trying to build a better queuing system with RabbitMQ if SQS does the trick.

Question Everything

I wish everyone was curious by nature—not only curious, but also interested in the inner working of things. If you are curious by nature, then you should regularly *browse* your AWS accounts looking for anomalies. This curiosity should be cultivated because there are interesting events happening all the time. The first thing we need to do is identify them, and then we can monitor for their occurrences.

If you question everything you can easily identify waste, which is something we categorically try to prevent.

Don't Waste

The more resources you have, the more they can (and will) fail. Start by minimizing the different types of resources. Why do you need Postgres and MySQL? Why do you need MongoDB and DynamoDB?

Don't waste your resources; make sure they do their fair share of work. Tune your instances for reliable operation (stay within the instance resources of CPU and memory). And always try to run the minimum amount of instances necessary.

Do not keep unused resources. Not only do they cost money but it is also more difficult to find problems with a lot of rubbish around. Services like Auto Scaling are free and force you to think about flexible resource allocation.

AWS is constantly looking to innovate in the space of resource utilization. They introduced Spot Instances, for example, to optimize utilization distribution by introducing a marketplace. You can bid on instances, which will be launched when the chosen price point is reached. Another example is Reduced Redundancy Storage with S3, less reliable but significantly cheaper. And very recently they introduced Glacier, a storage service like S3, but analogous to tape backups.

But, there is another, even more important reason to keep your nest clean. It is a much more pleasant place to work. It will feel like home to you and everyone else on your team.

Learn from Others

Learning starts with respect. Your colleagues often deal with similar problems. You might think your problems are the most difficult in the world. Well, they probably are not. Talk to your colleagues. Be honest and share your doubts and worries. They will tell you theirs. And together you will figure out how to deal with the next outage.

Amazon AWS forums

The Amazon AWS forums might be their most important asset. There are thousands of people discussing services and finding help for the problems they encounter.

If you can't find your answer directly, you will find many helpful people with potentially the same experience as you.

You Are Not Alone

Finally, make sure you build a team. Running operations, large or small, is difficult. Having everything under control makes this fun, but doing it together takes the edge off.

There are different *event streams* with more or less important bits of information. You can try to build a tool to sift out every meaningful bit. You can also rely on your team to use weak signals in all the noise. Outages and routine operational work is much more fun to do with your colleagues.

Remember, engineering is teamwork!

elasticsearch

Most of the technology stacks we use are not yet designed for the cloud. In Ubuntu (Linux) every so often you have to jump through hoops to get your root volume checked. Replication in most databases, synchronous or asynchronous, is notoriously hard to get right. And once running, scaling *up* resources takes an extreme amount of courage.

Most of these problems make your systems less resilient and reliable, because you just can't be flexible with resources.

elasticsearch is the first infrastructural component that gets it right. They really understand what it takes to operate datastores (it is much more than search). And therefore this is the first example we'll talk about.

Introduction

"It is an Open Source (Apache 2), Distributed, RESTful, Search Engine built on top of Apache Lucene."

The operational unit of elasticsearch is a cluster, not a server. Note that this is already different from many other datastore technologies. You can have a cluster of one, for development or test, or for transient data. But in production you will want to have at least two nodes most of the time.

elasticsearch holds json data in indexes. These indexes are broken up into shards. If you have a cluster with multiple nodes, shards are distributed in such a way that you can lose a node. You can manipulate almost everything in elasticsearch, so changing the sharding is not too difficult.

To add a document to an index (if the index doesn't exist it is created):

```
$ curl -XPOST 'http://elasticsearch.heystaq.com:9200/heystaq/snapshot/?pret-
ty=true' -d '{
```

```
    "scanId" : "Ibx9biARRAGX1ygl08Y4zQ",
        "region" : "eu-west-1",
        "snapshotId" : "snap-cc79c0a7",
        "status" : "completed",
        "capacity" : "50",
        "started" : "2012-04-25T06:00:17.000Z",
        "volumeId" : "vol-b268cada"
}'
{
  "ok" : true,
  "_index" : "heystaq",
  "_type" : "snapshot",
  "_id" : "7bQUFu_gT8CWyjLJXaupGg",
  "_version" : 1
}
```

An elasticsearch query can be fired at any node in the cluster. Smart clients are nodes themselves, without holding data. They *scout* the cluster and can use multiple nodes, all at their convenience. We do not know the practical upper limit in the number of nodes, but scaling like this is very easy.

Searching is just as easy:

```
$   curl   -XGET   'http://elasticsearch.heystaq.com:9200/heystaq/_search?pret-
ty=true' -d '{
    "sort" : [
        { "_timestamp" : { "order" : "desc" } }
    ],
    "from" : 0, "size" : 1,
    "query" : {
        "term" : { "snapshotId": "snap-cc79c0a7" }
    }
}'
{
  "took" : 187,
  "timed_out" : false,
  "_shards" : {
    "total" : 5,
    "successful" : 5,
    "failed" : 0
  },
  "hits" : {
    "total" : 216,
    "max_score" : null,
    "hits" : [ {
      "_index" : "heystaq",
      "_type" : "snapshot",
      "_id" : "7bQUFu_gT8CWyjLJXaupGg",
      "_score" : null,
      "_source" : {
        "scanId" : "Ibx9biARRAGX1ygl08Y4zQ",
        "region" : "eu-west-1",
```

```
        "snapshotId" : "snap-cc79c0a7",
        "status" : "completed",
        "capacity" : "50",
        "started" : "2012-04-25T06:00:17.000Z",
        "volumeId" : "vol-b268cada"
      },
      "sort" : [ 1348138249308 ]
    } ]
  }
}
```

So without too much effort, you have a resilient and reliable datastore out of the box. You can add and remove nodes without too much hassle. Data is stored safely and can be queried in a very versatile way.

We use elasticsearch as a replacement for SOLR. We use it to power distributed logging with logstash, in environments with hundreds of events per second. But we also use it as a Big Data solution.

EC2 Plug-in

elasticsearch comes with an EC2 plug-in. Normally nodes can discover their context, or their environment with multicast. They can look for elasticsearch nodes, with the same clustername. But in AWS (EC2) we don't have multicast. The solution is to use security groups, or tags. You can also restrict discovery to specify Availability Zones. With this plug-in you can also tell elasticsearch to store the index in S3. In case of real serious problems you can always restore from this location. Pretty cool!

Missing Features

elasticsearch is nearly perfect, in our opinion. However, we did add some functionality to our elasticsearch cluster AMIs.

Scaling up means using more resources, memory, and CPU. The default configuration on an elasticsearch node does not take the liberty to reserve a proportionate amount of available system memory. So that is what we do on launch. We added something like this in /etc/default/elasticsearch:

```
# they advise to use half the memory (need to test)
ES_HEAP_SIZE=$(($(/usr/bin/awk '/MemTotal/{print $2}' /proc/meminfo) / 2))k
```

Startup scripts

We install elasticsearch from the supplied .deb package (Debian/Ubuntu format). This package installs, among other things, a startup script and accompanying default settings. `/etc/default/elasticsearch` contains the default settings for the elasticsearch startup script (`/etc/init.d/elasticsearch`).

The other thing we added is Route 53. When joining a cluster (something that a client also does) it needs an entrypoint. Any cluster node will do, so it doesn't matter where to start. To make this easy we have each node add itself to a Route 53 WRR (weighted round robin) record.

Boto

We often work with Python when we script these solutions. The main reason is Boto, a complete and up-to-date Python interface to AWS.

Boto is not listed as an AWS SDK. But since Boto's creator (Mitch Garnaat) now works for AWS, we regard it as stable enough for production work.

See Python & AWS Cookbook (*http://oreil.ly/Python_AWS_CB*).

When we launch, we call this:

```
# Copyright (C) 2011, 2012 9apps B.V.
#
# This file is part of ES for AWS.
#
# ES for AWS is free software: you can redistribute it and/or modify
# it under the terms of the GNU General Public License as published by
# the Free Software Foundation, either version 3 of the License, or
# (at your option) any later version.
#
# ES for AWS is distributed in the hope that it will be useful,
# but WITHOUT ANY WARRANTY; without even the implied warranty of
# MERCHANTABILITY or FITNESS FOR A PARTICULAR PURPOSE.  See the
# GNU General Public License for more details.
#
# You should have received a copy of the GNU General Public License
# along with ES for AWS. If not, see <http://www.gnu.org/licenses/>.

import os, sys, json

import boto.utils

from route53 import Route53Zone
```

```
userdata = json.loads(boto.utils.get_instance_userdata())
metadata = boto.utils.get_instance_metadata()

if __name__ == '__main__':
    key = userdata["iam"]["security-credentials"]["elasticsearch-heystaq-com"]
["AccessKeyId"]
    secret = userdata["iam"]["security-credentials"]["elasticsearch-heystaq-
com"]["SecretAccessKey"]
    r53_zone = Route53Zone(userdata['hosted_zone_id'], key, secret)

    name = "{0}.{1}".format(userdata['name'], userdata['hosted_zo-
ne'].rstrip('.'))
    value = metadata['hostname']
    identifier = metadata['instance-id']

    try:
        r53_zone.create_record(name, value, identifier, 100)
    except:
        r53_zone.update_record(name, value, identifier, 100)
```

With the help of the following, it manages the Route 53 WRR record:

```
# Copyright (C) 2011, 2012 9apps B.V.
#
# This file is part of ES for AWS.
#
# ES for AWS is free software: you can redistribute it and/or modify
# it under the terms of the GNU General Public License as published by
# the Free Software Foundation, either version 3 of the License, or
# (at your option) any later version.
#
# ES for AWS is distributed in the hope that it will be useful,
# but WITHOUT ANY WARRANTY; without even the implied warranty of
# MERCHANTABILITY or FITNESS FOR A PARTICULAR PURPOSE.  See the
# GNU General Public License for more details.
#
# You should have received a copy of the GNU General Public License
# along with ES for AWS. If not, see <http://www.gnu.org/licenses/>.

import os, sys, json

from boto.route53.connection import Route53Connection
from boto.route53.record import ResourceRecordSets

class Route53Zone:
    def __init__(self, zone_id, key=None, secret=None):
        self.zone_id = zone_id

        # perhaps we use an IAM role (although we had some problems with
Route53 before)
        if key == None or secret == None:
            self.route53 = Route53Connection()
        else:
```

```python
        self.route53 = Route53Connection(key, secret)

    def create_record(self, name, value, identifier=None, weight=None):
        changes = ResourceRecordSets(self.route53, self.zone_id)

        change = changes.add_change("CREATE", name + ".", "CNAME", 60,
                                                      identifier=iden-
tifier, weight=weight)
        change.add_value(value)
        changes.commit()

    def update_record(self, name, value, identifier=None, weight=None):
        changes = ResourceRecordSets(self.route53, self.zone_id)

        # there is no real update, so we combine delete and create in change
request
        sets = self.route53.get_all_rrsets(self.zone_id, None)
        for rset in sets:
            if rset.name == name + "." and rset.identifier == identifier:
                previous_value = rset.resource_records[0]

                change = changes.add_change("DELETE", name + ".", "CNAME", 60,
                                                       identifier=identifier,
weight=weight)
                change.add_value(previous_value)

        change = changes.add_change("CREATE", name + ".", "CNAME", 60,
                                                      identifier=iden-
tifier, weight=weight)
        change.add_value(value)
        changes.commit()

    def delete_record(self, name, identifier=None, weight=None):
        changes = ResourceRecordSets(self.route53, self.zone_id)

        value = None
        # only delete when it exists, otherwise we get painful errors
        sets = self.route53.get_all_rrsets(self.zone_id, None)
        for rset in sets:
            if rset.name == name + "." and rset.identifier == identifier:
                value = rset.resource_records[0]

        if value != None:
            change = changes.add_change("DELETE", name + ".", "CNAME", 60,
                                                       identifier=identifi-
er, weight=weight)
            change.add_value(value)
            changes.commit()

if __name__ == '__main__':
```

```
# easy testing, use like this (requires environment variables)
#       python route53.py create_record id key access name value
r53_zone = Route53Zone(sys.argv[2], sys.argv[3], sys.argv[4])
print getattr(r53_zone, sys.argv[1])(*sys.argv[5:])
```

Conclusion

This is it! With no *real* work we have an extremely powerful NoSQL-type Big Data solution. Now the only thing to do is climb the learning curve of elasticsearch itself. There is so much potential in this solution, we discover something new every day.

## CHAPTER 6

Postgres

Ok, if we want to play with bricks, the we're going to have to build some. This section will show how we approach building flexible, default components that can be used again and again. We require predictable performance and reliable operations. We have to be able to rotate, clone, link, cluster, backup, restore—all in minutes.

Postgres is one of components that we work with every day. Postgres is an open source, scalable relational database system. (The name "Postgres" is actually a shortened form of PostgreSQL.) We'll discuss the tools we use (SimpleDB, Route 53) and show how we run Postgres to provide high availability. All of the source code is available on pgRDS on github (*https://github.com/9apps/pgRDS*).

As long as Amazon RDS does not support Postgres, there will be people struggling to get it running. The *official* lamenting to be heard online is that EBS sucks. EBS is said to be slow and unreliable in performance, for example.

As described before, EBS is a new storage technology. It is popularly described as something in between RAID and local disk storage. Because it is different, people have had unrealistic expectations of it. They are disappointed if performance fluctuatees, and start to call EBS unreliable. And they call EBS slow if hardware RAID or SSD feels faster.

But, if we focus on the opportunities EBS brings (many small volumes with sophisticated snapshot capabilities) we can solve this problem as well. We'll show that Postgres can be made to scale really well, combining the strengths of both Postgres and AWS.

IOPS EBS

AWS listens very well to their customers. They continuously innovate to solve problems people experience.

One of the problems is consistent I/O performance of EBS. They introduced Provisioned IOPS for Amazon EBS (*http://amzn.to/Vb4HRr*). You can now purchase a minimum amount guaranteed I/O operations per second.

This is important, but does not solve the absolute upper limit of a single EBS volume. Even with IOPS nothing beats the ability to scale out with many EBS volumes to solve these problems.

Pragmatism First

Our Postgres will span several database clusters, not hundreds of thousands. Our clusters have to be stable, of course. We want to be flexible with our datastores, so we need to be able to scale clusters easily in several ways. We also need a reliable restore to point in time, which we will use for cloning clusters.

Because our scope is *several clusters* there are a couple of things we do not yet implement:

1. Automatic failover (think multi Availability Zone RDS instance), due to time constraints.

2. Dynamic parameters (still in progress; RDS has Parameter Groups), since RDS handles failover within several minutes. With this Postgres solution, we add another two to three minutes for manual intervention.

Because we only have several clusters running, failure of a master database is very rare. Because we always plan to run with one or more slaves we can easily promote one manually. The consequence is that we add one or two minutes to a failover event.

Dynamic parameters is not a feature that is required often. We choose to run with a good set of default parameters. We do not want to master Postgres, we want to master our applications. If we can relatively easily replace cluster nodes we can also change Postgres parameters.

The Challenge

In our situation the biggest challenge is the disk space. The largest instances offer us up to 68GB of memory, which should be enough to work with. But we work with complicated schemas, a lot of data (hundreds of gigabytes), and many operations.

The way out of disk problems with databases is SSD (Solid State Drive) devices, but we don't have an SSD device. We could use a high I/O EBS volume, but that only alleviates the problem a little bit. The new high I/O quadruple extra large instance has 2TB of SSD-backed local storage. We could use that for temporary tables.

But in the end, SSD and high I/O volumes are a short-term solution when dealing with big databases. You want to be able to scale the storage horizontally.

Tablespaces

Well, as it turns out, Postgres has an *old* technology designed to scale the storage. We can use tablespaces to move tables and indexes to other filesystems. This is advertised for moving your one problematic table to a different type of storage like SSD. But we are on AWS; we have EBS. If we could easily work with tablespaces, we could spread our disk operations across many EBS volumes. So that is what we are going to do.

Alternative approach

An alternative approach to scaling storage horizontally is RAID. In this case we can't use it, because, as you will see later, engineering backup and restore functionality is very difficult.

Building Blocks

The basic building blocks we are going to use to create this Postgres component are:

- EC2
- S3
- SimpleDB
- Route 53
- CloudWatch

EC2 is an obvious choice because we need instances and volumes. We'll use S3 for the WAL archive files [files that help in restoring the database after a crash; for more on this, see "WAL Archive" (page 52)]. SimpleDB is handy for housekeeping. Route 53 will help us identify our resources. And CloudWatch is necessary to keep an eye on the entire operation.

Configuration with userdata

When we launch a node, it starts or joins a cluster. We are going to launch a master with userdata like this:

```
{
  "name"        : "db01",
  "cluster"     : "db.9apps.net",
  "slow"        : "500",
  "tablespaces" :
  [
    { "device" : "/dev/sdf", "name" : "main", "size" : 100}
  ]
}
```

To launch a slave, we would give userdata like this:

```
{
  "name"        : "db02",
  "cluster"     : "db.9apps.net",
  "master"      : "db01.9apps.net",
  "slow"        : "500",
  "tablespaces" :
  [
    { "device" : "/dev/sdf", "name" : "main", "size" : 100}
  ]
}
```

A clone can be launched like this (this will start a new cluster):

```
{
  "name"        : "db",
  "cluster"     : "development.9apps.net",
  "clone"       : "db01.9apps.net",
  "tablespaces" :
  [
    { "device" : "/dev/sdf", "name" : "main", "size" : 100}
  ]
}
```

This approach makes it very flexible to grow, as adding tablespaces is not extremely difficult. You simply specify an additional tablespace in the userdata, and rotate the cluster nodes. When the new nodes are launched, the existing tablespaces are ignored, or changed when we increase the size of the volume. If a tablespace didn't exist before, it is created. The full source of node provisioning looks like this:

```
# Copyright (C) 2011, 2012 9apps B.V.
#
# This file is part of pgRDS for AWS.
#
# pgRDS is free software: you can redistribute it and/or modify
# it under the terms of the GNU General Public License as published by
# the Free Software Foundation, either version 3 of the License, or
# (at your option) any later version.
#
# pgRDS is distributed in the hope that it will be useful,
# but WITHOUT ANY WARRANTY; without even the implied warranty of
# MERCHANTABILITY or FITNESS FOR A PARTICULAR PURPOSE.  See the
```

```
# GNU General Public License for more details.
#
# You should have received a copy of the GNU General Public License
# along with pgRDS. If not, see <http://www.gnu.org/licenses/>.

#
# Usage:
#        backup.py <cmd> EC2_KEY_ID EC2_SECRET_KEY <expiration>
#
# <cmd>: snapshot or purge
# <expiration>: hourly (default), daily, weekly, monthly
#

import os, sys, subprocess, json, psycopg2
from time import gmtime,strftime,time

import boto.utils, boto.ec2
from boto.ec2.connection import EC2Connection

import settings, administration

# OK, let's get some userdata and metadata
userdata = json.loads(boto.utils.get_user_data())
if not userdata.has_key('tablespaces'):
    userdata['tablespaces'] = [{ "device" : "/dev/sdf",
                                                    "name" : "main",
"size" : 2}]

metadata = boto.utils.get_instance_metadata()
instance_id = metadata['instance-id']
hostname = metadata['public-hostname']

# zone is not available directly (we assume the structure stays the same)
zone = metadata['placement']['availability-zone']
region = zone[:-1]

# expiration in the future, calculated like this
days = 24 * 60 * 60
form = "%Y-%m-%d %H:%M:%S"
expires = {'hourly': strftime(form, gmtime(time() + 7 * days)),
                 'daily': strftime(form, gmtime(time() + 14 * days)),
                 'weekly': strftime(form, gmtime(time() + 61 * days)),
                 'monthly': strftime(form, gmtime(time() + 365 * days))}

# snapshot a certain device, with a particular expiration
def make_snapshot(key, access, cluster, name="main", expiration='weekly',
                            device="/dev/sdf"):
    # first get the mountpoint (requires some energy, but we can...)
    df = subprocess.Popen(["/bin/df", device], stdout=subprocess.PIPE)
    output = df.communicate()[0]
      dummy, size, used, available, percent, mountpoint = output.split("\n")
[1].split()
```

```python
    ec2 = boto.ec2.connect_to_region(region, aws_access_key_id = key, aws_se-
cret_access_key = access)

    # if we have the device (/dev/sdf) just don't do anything anymore
    mapping = ec2.get_instance_attribute(instance_id, 'blockDeviceMapping')
    try:
        volume_id = mapping['blockDeviceMapping'][device].volume_id

        os.system("/usr/sbin/xfs_freeze -f {0}".format(mountpoint))
        snapshot = ec2.create_snapshot(volume_id,
                                "Backup of {0} - for {1}/{2} - expires
{3}".format(

volume_id, cluster, name,

expires[expiration]))
    except Exception as e:
        print e
    finally:
        os.system("/usr/sbin/xfs_freeze -u {0}".format(mountpoint))

    return ["{0}".format(snapshot.id), expires[expiration]]

# delete a number of snapshots
def purge_snapshots(key, access, cluster, snapshots):
    ec2 = boto.ec2.connect_to_region(region, aws_access_key_id = key, aws_se-
cret_access_key = access)

    for snapshot in snapshots:
        try:
            print "deleting snapshot: {0}".format(snapshot['snapshot'])
            ec2.delete_snapshot(snapshot['snapshot'])
        except:
            pass

            administration.delete_snapshot(key, access, cluster,snapshot['snap-
shot'])

# actually the only thing this does is 'mark' the start
def start_backup(label):
    conn = psycopg2.connect(host=settings.host, dbname=settings.database_name,
                                            user=settings.database_user,
                                            password=settings.data-
base_password)
    try:
        conn.autocommit = True
        cur = conn.cursor()

        cur.execute('select pg_start_backup(\x27{0}\x27)'.format(label))
    finally:
        cur.close()
```

```
        conn.close()

# and, 'mark' the stop
def stop_backup():
    conn = psycopg2.connect(host=settings.host, dbname=settings.database_name,
                                             user=settings.database_user,
                                             password=settings.data-
base_password)

    try:
        conn.autocommit = True
        cur = conn.cursor()

        cur.execute("select pg_stop_backup()")
    finally:
        cur.close()
        conn.close()

def is_in_recovery():
    conn = psycopg2.connect(host=settings.host, dbname=settings.database_name,
                                             user=settings.database_user,
                                             password=settings.data-
base_password)
    try:
        conn.autocommit = True
        cur = conn.cursor()

        cur.execute("select pg_is_in_recovery()")
        in_recovery = cur.fetchone()[0]
    finally:
        cur.close()
        conn.close()

    return in_recovery == True

# for convenience we can call this file to make backups directly
if __name__ == '__main__':
    # get the bucket, from the name
    name = userdata['name'].strip()
    hosted_zone = os.environ['HOSTED_ZONE_NAME'].rstrip('.')
    name = "{0}.{1}".format(name, hosted_zone)
    cluster = userdata['cluster'].strip()

    def snapshot_all(expiration="weekly", master=True):
        # don't snapshot the WAL or root volume
        for tablespace in userdata['tablespaces']:
            backup = make_snapshot(sys.argv[2], sys.argv[3], cluster, table-
space['name'],
                                                          expiration=expira-
tion,
                                                          device=table-
space['device'])
```

```
                # we use "dummy" to make sure the backups are restored from
                if not master:
                        administration.add_snapshot(sys.argv[2], sys.argv[3], cluster,
    "dummy", backup)
                else:
                        administration.add_snapshot(sys.argv[2], sys.argv[3],
                                                            cluster, table-
    space['name'], backup)
                print "created {0} from {1}".format(backup[0], tablespace['name'])

        if "latest" == sys.argv[1]:
            print administration.get_latest_snapshot(sys.argv[2], sys.argv[3], clus-
    ter, sys.argv[4])
        elif "basebackup" == sys.argv[1]:
            if not is_in_recovery():
                start_backup(sys.argv[4])
                snapshot_all()
                stop_backup()
            else:
                snapshot_all("hourly", False)
        elif "snapshot" == sys.argv[1]:
            backup = make_snapshot(sys.argv[2], sys.argv[3],
                                                    cluster, sys.argv[4],
    sys.argv[5])
            administration.add_snapshot(sys.argv[2], sys.argv[3],
                                                    cluster, sys.argv[4],
    backup)
        elif "snapshot-all" == sys.argv[1]:
            snapshot_all()
        elif "purge" == sys.argv[1]:
            snapshots = administration.get_expired_snapshots(sys.argv[2],
    sys.argv[3], cluster)
            purge_snapshots(sys.argv[2], sys.argv[3], cluster, snapshots)

        elif "purge-all" == sys.argv[1]:
            snapshots = administration.get_all_snapshots(sys.argv[2],
    sys.argv[3], name)
            purge_snapshots(sys.argv[2], sys.argv[3], name, snapshots)
```

IAM Policies (Identity and Access Management)

We are going to use several AWS services that we need programmatic access to. We want to protect our systems from outside prying eyes, but we also want to protect ourselves from making costly mistakes. We use IAM to grant access to those assets and operations we need.

Creating IAM policies

Creating IAM policies is cumbersome at best. Most often this is pretty frustrating business. Most of the time we document our stuff relatively well, and copy/paste to our hearts content. If we need something new we always build this with AWS's Policy Generator (*http://bit.ly/ZTX4X3*) in combination with the developer or API guides.

Here are the policies that selectively grant necessary rights:

EC2

The EC2 policy is a bit too liberal, but in this case we have no choice. You can specify a particular instance resource in an IAM policy. But you can't specify *me* as a resource. This means scripts on instances can perform actions on all resources. It would be great if you could restrict actions on volumes to only those volumes that are attached to the instance, but you can't.

```
{
  "Statement": [
    {
      "Sid": "Stmt1327831658328",
      "Action": [
        "ec2:AttachVolume",
        "ec2:CreateSnapshot",
        "ec2:CreateTags",
        "ec2:CreateVolume",
        "ec2:DeleteSnapshot",
        "ec2:DeleteTags",
        "ec2:DeleteVolume",
        "ec2:DescribeInstanceAttribute",
        "ec2:DescribeSnapshots",
        "ec2:DescribeTags",
        "ec2:DescribeVolumes",
        "ec2:DetachVolume",
        "ec2:ModifyInstanceAttribute",
        "ec2:ResetInstanceAttribute"
      ],
      "Effect": "Allow",
      "Resource": [
        "*"
      ]
    }
  ]
}
```

S3

For S3 it is easier. We can use wildcards to give access to all buckets starting with *postgres*.

```
{
  "Statement": [
    {
      "Sid": "Stmt1346312055951",
      "Action": [
        "s3:*"
      ],
      "Effect": "Allow",
      "Resource": [
        "arn:aws:s3:::postgres*",
        "arn:aws:s3:::postgres*/*"
      ]
    }
  ]
}
```

SimpleDB

Here we chose a different approach. With S3 we assumed that the buckets have already been created. With SimpleDB we'll create them when they don't exist.

```
{
  "Statement": [
    {
      "Sid": "Stmt1328015970799",
      "Action": [
        "sdb:BatchDeleteAttributes",
        "sdb:BatchPutAttributes",
        "sdb:CreateDomain",
        "sdb:DeleteAttributes",
        "sdb:DomainMetadata",
        "sdb:GetAttributes",
        "sdb:ListDomains",
        "sdb:PutAttributes",
        "sdb:Select"
      ],
      "Effect": "Allow",
      "Resource": [
        "*"
      ]
    }
  ]
}
```

Route 53

We use one hosted zone only, to create different identifiers for (groups of) nodes.

```
{
  "Statement": [
    {
```

```
      "Sid": "Stmt1327831880545",
      "Action": [
        "route53:ChangeResourceRecordSets",
        "route53:GetHostedZone",
        "route53:ListHostedZones",
        "route53:ListResourceRecordSets"
      ],
      "Effect": "Allow",
      "Resource": [
        "arn:aws:route53:::hostedzone/Z148QEXAMPLE8V"
      ]
    }
  ]
}
```

CloudWatch

For monitoring cluster and node health:

```
{
  "Statement": [
    {
      "Sid": "Stmt1337411999556",
      "Action": [
        "cloudwatch:PutMetricData"
      ],
      "Effect": "Allow",
      "Resource": [
        "*"
      ]
    }
  ]
}
```

Postgres Persistence (backup/restore)

Remember that one of our goals is decent restore to point-in-time functionality. *Decent* with big databases is to be able to restore a full database with a copy of the data from several minutes ago. We could aim for seconds, but the additional cost does not warrant this investment.

As with Amazon RDS, we are going to work with the concept of full backup. In Postgres terms, this is called a basebackup, marked with *pg_start_backup* and *pg_stop_backup*. In addition to this we are going to persist the WAL archive to S3.

A full backup is not a dump; it is a collection of snapshots taken of the EBS volumes. A restore will create volumes from these snapshots, and will replay the WAL archive until the database is fully restored (to the latest version, or restored to a specific timestamp).

The full code of our backup script is as follows:

```
# Copyright (C) 2011, 2012 9apps B.V.
#
# This file is part of pgRDS for AWS.
#
# pgRDS for AWS is free software: you can redistribute it and/or modify
# it under the terms of the GNU General Public License as published by
# the Free Software Foundation, either version 3 of the License, or
# (at your option) any later version.
#
# pgRDS for AWS is distributed in the hope that it will be useful,
# but WITHOUT ANY WARRANTY; without even the implied warranty of
# MERCHANTABILITY or FITNESS FOR A PARTICULAR PURPOSE. See the
# GNU General Public License for more details.
#
# You should have received a copy of the GNU General Public License
# along with pgRDS for AWS. If not, see <http://www.gnu.org/licenses/>.

import os, sys, json

import boto.utils, boto.ec2
from boto.ec2.connection import EC2Connection

from route53 import Route53Zone

import settings

userdata = json.loads(boto.utils.get_user_data())
if not userdata.has_key('tablespaces'):
        userdata['tablespaces'] = [{ "device" : "/dev/sdf", "name" : "main",
"size" : 2}]

metadata = boto.utils.get_instance_metadata()
instance_id = metadata['instance-id']
hostname = metadata['public-hostname']

zone = metadata['placement']['availability-zone']
region = zone[:-1]

zone_name = os.environ['HOSTED_ZONE_NAME']
zone_id = os.environ['HOSTED_ZONE_ID']

pg_dir = '/var/lib/postgresql/9.1/'

import psycopg2

def pgbouncer():
    os.system("""sudo -u postgres psql -t -c
\"select '\\\"'||rolname||'\\\"'||' \\\"'||rolpassword||'\\\"'
from pg_authid ;\" | sed 's/^\s*//' | sed '/^$/d' > /etc/pgbouncer/user-
list.txt""")
    os.system("/etc/init.d/pgbouncer restart")
```

```python
def monitor():
    os.system("/usr/sbin/monit reload")
    os.system("/usr/sbin/monit monitor postgresql")

def create_tablespace(tablespace, location=None):
    conn = psycopg2.connect(host=settings.host, dbname=settings.database_name,
                                                user=settings.database_user,
                                                password=settings.data-
base_password)
    try:
        conn.autocommit = True
        cur = conn.cursor()
        if location == None or location == "":
            location = "{0}{1}".format(pg_dir, tablespace)

            cur.execute('CREATE TABLESPACE {0} LOCATION \x27{1}\x27'.format(table-
space, location))
    finally:
        cur.close()
        conn.close()

def alter_table_set_tablespace(table, tablespace):
    conn = psycopg2.connect(host=settings.host, dbname=settings.database_name,
                                                user=settings.database_user,
                                                password=settings.data-
base_password)
    try:
        cur = conn.cursor()

        cur.execute('ALTER TABLE {0} SET TABLESPACE {1}'.format(table, table-
space))
        conn.commit()
    finally:
        cur.close()
        conn.close()

# without a root database and root user we have nothing
def prepare_database():
    os.system('sudo -u postgres psql -c "create user root"')
    os.system('sudo -u postgres psql -c "create database root"')
    os.system('sudo -u postgres psql -c "grant all on database root to root"')
    os.system('sudo -u postgres psql -c "alter user {0} password
\x27{1}\x27"'.format(
                                                settings.database_user,set-
tings.database_password))

if __name__ == '__main__':
    ec2 = boto.ec2.connect_to_region(region, aws_access_key_id = sys.argv[1],
                            aws_secret_access_key = sys.argv[2])
    r53_zone = Route53Zone(sys.argv[1], sys.argv[2], zone_id)
```

```
                name    =    "{0}.{1}".format(userdata['name'],os.environ['HOS-
TED_ZONE_NAME'].rstrip('.'))

    if sys.argv[3] == "start":
        # make sure others can check on us (logfiles)
        os.system('chmod 644 /var/log/postgresql/*.log')
        # don't hijack the record, but do continue
        try:
            r53_zone.create_record(name, hostname)
        except:
            pass
        ec2.create_tags([instance_id], { "Name": name })

        # we only prepare the database when we are NOT subservient
        if 'master' in userdata:
            prepare_database()

        pgbouncer()
        monitor()
    elif sys.argv[3] == "tablespaces":
        for tablespace in userdata['tablespaces']:
            name = tablespace['name']
            if name != "main":
                try:
                    create_tablespace(name)
                except:
                    print "tablespace {0} already exists?".format(name)

                try:
                    alter_table_set_tablespace(name, name)
                except:
                    print "table {0} does not exist yet?".format(name)
```

WAL Archive

Postgres has a feature called "write ahead logging" (WAL). These WAL files maintain a continuous backup of log files which help in restoring the database after a system crash. Postgres's own description is clear as to the intent of the developers of this feature.

"One aspect of reliable operation is that all data recorded by a committed transaction should be stored in a nonvolatile area that is safe from power loss, operating system failure, and hardware failure (except failure of the nonvolatile area itself, of course)."

When enabling WAL files, you can also have these files archived. This is what we use to enable point-in-time restores (the master has WAL enabled and archived to S3):

```
archive_mode = on
archive_command = '/usr/bin/s3cmd -c /etc/postgresql/.s3cfg put %p s3://9apps-
net/%f'
archive_timeout = 60
```

A restore looks like this:

```
restore_command  =  '/usr/bin/s3cmd  -c  /etc/postgresql/.s3cfg  get  s3://9apps-
net/%f %p'
```

All of this is fully automated depending on userdata and the state of the cluster.

When doing a restore to a point in time for the sake of making a copy, you want to tell the node to stop at a certain *point in time.* By default, when you omit the timestamp userdata, the restore will try to get as far as possible, after which is stops restoring.

In Practice

We run Postgres clusters with over 10 tablespaces. A basebackup takes about an hour to complete, but that is entirely dependent on the size and level of activity of the EBS volumes. Usually a basebackup does not interfere too much with normal operations, but it is a good idea to run this when traffic is not at its peak.

This cluster had one master and two slaves. Both of these slaves were serving reads, and both were *hot* enough to take over the master when necessary.

Self Reliance

In this Postgres cluster approach, we choose self reliance as our mode of operations. What we mean by that is that we have no outside *puppet master* that pulls the strings. The instances themselves determine the necessary course of action. And in case they don't know what to do, there is always human intervention.

Pragmatic automation

Some say that whatever needs to be done more than two times needs to be automated. This sounds nice, but it is ridiculously absurd when you think of it.

Some tasks are just too critical to automate 100%, like initiating a deploy to production. Sometimes it is more economical to perform some tasks manually because automating is just too expensive.

Automation is fun, sure. But it doesn't necessarily make your apps more reliable or resilient. And in the end, that is what matters.

The core of this self reliance is an AMI (Amazon Machine Image). An AMI is like a boot CD. It contains the root image with everything necessary to start an instance, so when an instance is launched it has basically everything already installed. We do not install software when instances are launched because we always try to minimize the possibility of unintended consequences.

Our AMI holds an Ubuntu LTS install and Postgres. We install Postgres something like this:

```
# postgres
$ add-apt-repository ppa:pitti/postgresql
$ apt-get update

$ apt-get install postgresql-9.1 postgresql-client-9.1 pgtune
```

We can't stress this enough: you should always choose a proven install method and do your best to keep everything as default as possible.

Once Postgres is running, you can use Monit to keep it in check:

```
check process postgresql with pidfile /var/run/postgresql/9.1-main.pid
    start program = "/etc/init.d/postgresql start"
    stop  program = "/etc/init.d/postgresql stop"
     if failed unixsocket /var/run/postgresql/.s.PGSQL.5432 protocol pgsql then
restart
     if failed unixsocket /var/run/postgresql/.s.PGSQL.5432 protocol pgsql then
alert
    if failed host localhost port 5432 protocol pgsql then restart
    if failed host localhost port 5432 protocol pgsql then alert
    if 5 restarts within 5 cycles then timeout
    group database
```

Postgres is launched from the default `/etc/init.d/postgres` script. In this script we intervene for provisioning (see configure.py), starting and stopping.

Working with AMIs is the most tedious task of all, but it is also the most important. You need to be able to rely on your AMI to work, especially in circumstances where you need it the most. Because there is no AMI simulator, you can test it only by launching new instances.

Monitoring

You probably got the idea of how we run Postgres. We have used RDS as a role model, while keeping in mind the practical constraints we are working under. There is one very important aspect to running infrastructural components like a database: we need to be able to monitor and send alerts when certain events occur. We use CloudWatch for that.

Again, we choose the self reliant approach. Every node reports on itself and what it knows about the cluster. We let CloudWatch handle the aggregation of the metrics collected.

The full monitor.py script is as follows:

```
# Copyright (C) 2011, 2012 9apps B.V.
#
# This file is part of Redis for AWS.
#
# Redis for AWS is free software: you can redistribute it and/or modify
# it under the terms of the GNU General Public License as published by
# the Free Software Foundation, either version 3 of the License, or
```

```
# (at your option) any later version.
#
# Redis for AWS is distributed in the hope that it will be useful,
# but WITHOUT ANY WARRANTY; without even the implied warranty of
# MERCHANTABILITY or FITNESS FOR A PARTICULAR PURPOSE.  See the
# GNU General Public License for more details.
#
# You should have received a copy of the GNU General Public License
# along with Redis for AWS. If not, see <http://www.gnu.org/licenses/>.


import os, sys, json, hashlib
import psycopg2, psycopg2.extras

from datetime import datetime

import boto.utils, boto.ec2, boto.ec2.cloudwatch

import settings

#
# pgRDS MONITOR
#
#
class Monitor:
    def __init__(self, key, access):
        self.userdata = json.loads(boto.utils.get_instance_userdata())
        self.metadata = boto.utils.get_instance_metadata()

        public_hostname = self.metadata['public-hostname']
        zone = self.metadata['placement']['availability-zone']
        region = zone[:-1]

        # the name (and identity) of the cluster (the master)
        self.cluster = self.userdata['cluster']
        self.name = "{0}.{1}".format(self.userdata['name'], self.cluster)

        self.cloudwatch = boto.ec2.cloudwatch.connect_to_region(region,
                        aws_access_key_id = key,
                        aws_secret_access_key = access)
        self.namespace = '9apps/postgres'

        self.connection = psycopg2.connect(host=settings.host,
                                                port=5432,
                                                    dbname=settings.data-
base_name,
                                                        user=settings.data-
base_user,
                                                    password=settings.data-
base_password)

        # now, the non-system database connections
```

```python
        self.databases = []
        try:
            database_cursor = self.connection.cursor()

            database_cursor.execute("select datname from pg_stat_database where
datname !~ '(template[0-9]+|root|postgres)'")
            for database in database_cursor:
                self.databases.append([database[0],
                                                psycopg2.connect(host=set-
tings.host, port=5432,
                                                dbname=database[0], user=set-
tings.database_user,
                                                password=settings.database_pass-
word)])
        finally:
            database_cursor.close()

        self.pgbouncer = psycopg2.connect(host=settings.host,
                                          port=6432,
                                          dbname='pgbouncer',
                                                user=settings.data-
base_user,
                                          password=settings.data-
base_password)
        # without this it doesn't work
        self.pgbouncer.set_isolation_level(0)

    def __del__(self):
        self.connection.close()

    def is_in_recovery(self):
        self.connection.autocommit = True

        try:
            cur = self.connection.cursor()

            cur.execute("select pg_is_in_recovery()")
            in_recovery = cur.fetchone()[0]
        finally:
            cur.close()

        return in_recovery == True

    def collect(self, monitoring = 'on'):
        if monitoring not in ['on', 'all']:
            return [[], [], [], {}]

        now = datetime.utcnow()

        names = []
        values = []
        units = []
```

```
            dimensions = { 'name' : self.name,
                           'cluster' : self.cluster }

        if 'master' in self.userdata:
            [offset, receive_offset, replay_offset] = self._get_standby_lag()

            if receive_offset != None:
                names.append('receive_lag')
                values.append(int(offset - receive_offset))
                units.append('Bytes')

            if replay_offset != None:
                names.append('replay_lag')
                values.append(int(offset - replay_offset))
                units.append('Bytes')

        for database in self.databases:
            for relation in ["heap", "idx"]:
                [read, hit, hitratio] = self._get_hitratio(database[1], rela-
tion)

                names.append("{0}_{1}_read".format(database[0], relation))
                values.append(int(read))
                units.append("Count")

                names.append("{0}_{1}_hit".format(database[0], relation))
                values.append(int(hit))
                units.append("Count")

                if hitratio != None:
                    names.append("{0}_{1}_hitratio".format(database[0], rela-
tion))
                    values.append(float(hitratio * 100))
                    units.append("Percent")

            conflicts = self._get_conflicts(database[0])
            names.append("{0}_{1}".format(database[0], 'confl_tablespace'))
            values.append(int(conflicts[0]))
            units.append("Count")

            names.append("{0}_{1}".format(database[0], 'confl_lock'))
            values.append(int(conflicts[1]))
            units.append("Count")

            names.append("{0}_{1}".format(database[0], 'confl_snapshot'))
            values.append(int(conflicts[2]))
            units.append("Count")

            names.append("{0}_{1}".format(database[0], 'confl_bufferpin'))
            values.append(int(conflicts[3]))
            units.append("Count")
```

```
                names.append("{0}_{1}".format(database[0], 'confl_deadlock'))
                values.append(int(conflicts[4]))
                units.append("Count")

                indexes_size = self._get_indexes_size(database[1])
                names.append("{0}_indexes_size".format(database[0]))
                values.append(int(indexes_size))
                units.append("Bytes")

                tables_size = self._get_tables_size(database[1])
                names.append("{0}_tables_size".format(database[0]))
                values.append(int(tables_size))
                units.append("Bytes")

        # nr of wal files
        size = self._get_nr_wal_files()
        names.append("wal_files")
        values.append(int(size))
        units.append("Count")

        # pgbouncer stats
        stats = self._get_pgbouncer_stats()
        names.append("pgbouncer_avg_req")
        values.append(int(stats[0]))
        units.append("Count/Second")

        names.append("pgbouncer_avg_recv")
        values.append(int(stats[1]))
        units.append("Bytes/Second")

        names.append("pgbouncer_avg_sent")
        values.append(int(stats[2]))
        units.append("Bytes/Second")

        names.append("pgbouncer_avg_query")
        values.append(float(stats[3] / 1000000))
        units.append("Seconds")

        # pgbouncer pools
        pools = self._get_pgbouncer_pools()
        names.append("pgbouncer_cl_active")
        values.append(float(pools[0]))
        units.append("Count")

        names.append("pgbouncer_cl_waiting")
        values.append(float(pools[1]))
        units.append("Count")

        names.append("pgbouncer_sv_active")
        values.append(float(pools[2]))
        units.append("Count")
```

```python
        names.append("pgbouncer_sv_idle")
        values.append(float(pools[3]))
        units.append("Count")

        names.append("pgbouncer_sv_used")
        values.append(float(pools[4]))
        units.append("Count")

        names.append("pgbouncer_sv_tested")
        values.append(float(pools[5]))
        units.append("Count")

        names.append("pgbouncer_sv_login")
        values.append(float(pools[6]))
        units.append("Count")

        names.append("pgbouncer_maxwait")
        values.append(float(pools[7]))
        units.append("Count")

        return [names, values, units, dimensions]

    def put(self):
        result = False
        try:
            # only monitor if we are told to (this will break, if not set)
            monitoring = self.userdata['monitoring']
        except:
            monitoring = 'on'

        if monitoring in ['on', 'all']:
            # first get all we need
            [names, values, units, dimensions] = self.collect(monitoring)
            while len(names) > 0:
                names20 = names[:20]
                values20 = values[:20]
                units20 = units[:20]

                # we can't send all at once, only 20 at a time
                # first aggregated over all
                result = self.cloudwatch.put_metric_data(self.namespace,
                                            names20, value=values20,
unit=units20)
                for dimension in dimensions:
                    dimension = { dimension : dimensions[dimension] }
                    result &= self.cloudwatch.put_metric_data(
                                        self.namespace, names20, value=val-
ues20,
                                        unit=units20, dimensions=dimension)

                del names[:20]
                del values[:20]
```

```
                del units[:20]
        else:
            print "we are not monitoring"

        return result

    def metrics(self):
        return self.cloudwatch.list_metrics()

    def _get_nr_wal_files(self):
        try:
            cursor = self.connection.cursor()

            sql = "select count(name) from (select pg_ls_dir('pg_xlog') as
name) as xlogs where name != 'archive_status'"
            cursor.execute(sql)

            [size] = cursor.fetchone()
        finally:
            cursor.close()

        return size

    def _get_tables_size(self, connection):
        try:
            cursor = connection.cursor()

            sql = "select sum(pg_relation_size(relid)) from pg_stat_user_tables"
            cursor.execute(sql)

            [size] = cursor.fetchone()
        finally:
            cursor.close()

        return size

    def _get_indexes_size(self, connection):
        try:
            cursor = connection.cursor()

                    sql = "select sum(pg_relation_size(indexrelid)) from
pg_stat_user_indexes"
            cursor.execute(sql)

            [size] = cursor.fetchone()
        finally:
            cursor.close()

        return size

    def _get_conflicts(self, database):
        try:
```

```
        cursor = self.connection.cursor()

            sql = "select * from pg_stat_database_conflicts where datname =
    '{0}'".format(database)
            cursor.execute(sql)

            conflicts = cursor.fetchone()
        finally:
            cursor.close()

        return [conflicts[2], conflicts[3], conflicts[4],
                        conflicts[5], conflicts[6]]

    def _get_hitratio(self, connection, relation="heap"):
        if relation == "heap":
            table = "tables"
        else:
            table = "indexes"

        try:
            cursor = connection.cursor()

            sql = "select sum({0}_blks_read) as read, sum({0}_blks_hit) as hit,
    (sum({0}_blks_hit) - sum({0}_blks_read)) / nullif(sum({0}_blks_hit),0) as hitra-
    tio from pg_statio_user_{1}".format(relation, table)
            cursor.execute(sql)

            [read, hit, hitratio] = cursor.fetchone()
        finally:
            cursor.close()

        return [read, hit, hitratio]

    def _get_standby_lag(self):
        try:
            master = psycopg2.connect(host=self.userdata['master'],
                                      dbname=settings.database_name,
                                      user=settings.database_user,
                                      password=settings.database_password)

            master.autocommit = True
            try:
                cursor = master.cursor()
                cursor.execute( "SELECT pg_current_xlog_location() AS location")
                [x, y] = (cursor.fetchone()[0]).split('/')
                offset = (int('ff000000', 16) * int(x, 16)) + int(y, 16)
            finally:
                cursor.close()

            try:
                cursor = self.connection.cursor()
```

```python
                    cursor.execute( "SELECT pg_last_xlog_receive_location(),
pg_last_xlog_replay_location()")
                one = cursor.fetchone()

                try:
                    [x, y] = (one[0]).split('/')
                        receive_offset = (int('ff000000', 16) * int(x, 16)) +
int(y, 16)
                except:
                    receive_offset = None

                try:
                    [x, y] = (one[1]).split('/')
                    replay_offset = (int('ff000000', 16) * int(x, 16)) + int(y,
16)
                except:
                    replay_offset = None
            finally:
                cursor.close()
        finally:
            master.close()

        return [offset, receive_offset, replay_offset]

    def _get_pgbouncer_stats(self):
        try:
            cursor = self.pgbouncer.cursor()
            cursor.execute('show stats')

            # ('pgbouncer\x00', 119L, 0L, 0L, 0L, 0L, 0L, 0L, 0L)
            [name, total_requests, total_received,
                total_sent, total_query_time, avg_req,
                avg_recv, avg_sent, avg_query] = cursor.fetchone()
        finally:
            cursor.close()

        return [avg_req, avg_recv, avg_sent, avg_query]

    def _get_pgbouncer_pools(self):
        cl_active = cl_waiting = sv_active = sv_idle = 0
        sv_used = sv_tested = sv_login = maxwait = 0
        try:
            cursor = self.pgbouncer.cursor()
            cursor.execute('show pools')

            # ('pgbouncer\x00', 'pgbouncer\x00', 1, 0, 0, 0, 0, 0, 0, 0)
            for pool in cursor:
                cl_active += pool[2]
                cl_waiting += pool[3]
                sv_active += pool[4]
                sv_idle += pool[5]
                sv_used += pool[6]
```

```
                    sv_tested += pool[7]
                    sv_login += pool[8]
                    maxwait = max(maxwait, pool[9])
            finally:
                cursor.close()

            return [cl_active, cl_waiting, sv_active, sv_idle,
                                    sv_used, sv_tested, sv_login, maxwait]

    if __name__ == '__main__':
        key = os.environ['EC2_KEY_ID']
        access = os.environ['EC2_SECRET_KEY']

        # easy testing, use like this (requires environment variables)
        #       python cluster.py get_master cluster 2c922342a.cluster
        monitor = Monitor(key, access)
        print getattr(monitor, sys.argv[1])(*sys.argv[3:])
```

We call this every minute, with a simple `cron` job.

Conclusion

This approach creates an RDS-like solution for Postgres. We do not need all the features of RDS, because they are not necessary or are too expensive. But we do have a very resilient and reliable Postgres that:

- Scales really well
- Is configurable
- Is easy to operate
- Is easily monitored

There are a few things that would be nice to have, such as automatic failover and master-master replication. But we'll add those features when the need arises.

## CHAPTER 7

MongoDB

MongoDB is one of the more prominent NoSQL databases at this time. In our MongoDB implementations the requirements are that of an *old-fashioned* database:

- Backup/restore
- Easy (horizontal) scalability
- Resilience to external influence
- Reliability

You can find the entire project on github (*https://github.com/9apps/mongodb*).

How It Works

For those who are new to MongoDB we'll briefly introduce the key concepts with their implementation. We work with MongoDB Replica Set for high availability. We'll use Route 53 to make sure it can be reached. We'll use SimpleDB for backup administration. And we'll use Amazon SQS (Simple Queue Service) for a simple task queue.

Replica Set

The high-availability version of MongoDB is called a Replica Set (Figure 7-1). In short, this is a collection of nodes, some of which hold data (members), and of those nodes holding data, one is master. The group uses a voting process to determine the master if there isn't one or if the current one is not healthy anymore. Nondata member nodes are called arbiters.

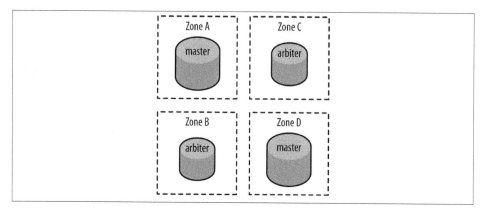

Figure 7-1. MongDB Replica Set

A Replica Set is only operational if the *majority is up*. For instance, if you have three Availability Zones, you need at least three nodes: two members holding data and one arbiter. Keep in mind that if you lose an entire Availability Zone, you want to keep an operational Replica Set.

Set configuration

We are lucky that elections are part of MongoDB. We don't have to worry about failover anymore, but we do have to configure Replica Sets. Members and arbiters should join a Replica Set automatically, and they should leave it in good state when they shut down.

We have two possible scenarios: one where the Replica Set doesn't exist yet and one where the set exists but has to be joined. The first case is relatively easy, because we only have to work on ourselves. The second is harder, because we have to task the master with adding us.

We join or initiate the cluster directly after the MongoDB daemon is launched. The replica set might be recovering or doing something else important first so telling the master to join directly at this point won't work. We use SQS to create a task queue.

The script for launching MongoDB shows how we handle this:

```
# Ubuntu upstart file at /etc/init/mongodb.conf

limit nofile 20000 20000
kill timeout 10

pre-start script
  # we do this in monit.conf as well, but we can't wait for that
  curl="curl --retry 3 --silent --show-error --fail"
      hostname_public=$($curl    http://169.254.169.254/latest/meta-data/public-
hostname)
  echo "host name = ["$hostname_public"]"
```

```
  hostname $hostname_public
  echo $hostname_public > /etc/hostname

  mkdir -p /var/mongodb/run
  chown -R mongodb.mongodb /var/mongodb/run

  arbiter=$(/root/is_arbiter.sh)
  if [ "x$arbiter" = "xno" ]; then
    /root/create_mongodb_volume.sh

    new=$(/root/new_set.sh)
    # if we are new, make sure we start without previous replica set conf
    if [ "x$new" = "xyes" ]; then
      rm -rf /var/mongodb/lib/local.*
    fi
  else
          rm -rf /var/mongodb/lib/ /var/mongodb/log /mnt/mongodb/log /var/run/
mongodb
  fi

  mkdir -p /var/mongodb/lib /var/run/mongodb /var/mongodb/log /mnt/mongodb/log
  chown -R mongodb.mongodb /var/run/mongodb /var/mongodb /mnt/mongodb/log

  /root/init-backups
end script

post-start script
  # wait for activity on port 27017
  while ! nc -q0 localhost 27017 </dev/null >/dev/null 2>&1; do
    sleep 1;
  done

  arbiter=$(/root/is_arbiter.sh)
  if [ "x$arbiter" = "xno" ]; then
    # we might be initial member of a new replica set
    new=$(/root/new_set.sh)

    # if we are, initiate the set, if not tell the primary we want to be part
    if [ "x$new" = "xyes" ]; then
      echo $(/usr/bin/mongo --eval "rs.initiate()") >> /var/log/syslog
    else
      task="\"rs.add('`hostname`:27017')\""
      /root/add_task.sh "${task}"
    fi

    # add the full crontab
    /bin/cat /root/crontab | /usr/bin/crontab -
  else
    task="\"rs.addArb('`hostname`:27017')\""
    /root/add_task.sh "${task}"

    # arbiter does nothing, or relatively very little
```

```
      /bin/cat /dev/null | /usr/bin/crontab -
    fi
  end script

  pre-stop script
    /usr/bin/mongo --eval "if( rs.isMaster()) { rs.stepDown()}"

    # schedule us to be removed (by the primary)
    task="\"rs.remove('`hostname`:27017')\""
    /root/add_task.sh "${task}"
  end script

  start on runlevel [2345]
  stop on runlevel RUNLEVEL=0 PREVLEVEL=2

  script
    curl="curl --retry 3 --silent --show-error --fail"
    set_name=$($curl http://169.254.169.254/latest/user-data | grep '"name"' |
sed 's/.*\:[ \t]*"\{0,1\}\([^,"]*\)"\{0,1\},\{0,1\}/\1/')


    ENABLE_MONGODB="yes"
    if [ -f /etc/default/mongodb ]; then . /etc/default/mongodb; fi
    if [ "x$ENABLE_MONGODB" = "xyes" ]; then
      arbiter=$(/root/is_arbiter.sh)
      if [ "x$arbiter" = "xno" ]; then
        exec start-stop-daemon --start --make-pidfile --pidfile /var/run/mongodb/
mongodb.pid --chuid mongodb --exec  /usr/bin/mongod -- --rest --oplogSize 5120
--config /etc/mongodb.conf --replSet $set_name;
      else
        exec start-stop-daemon --start --make-pidfile --pidfile /var/run/mongodb/
mongodb.pid --chuid mongodb --exec  /usr/bin/mongod -- --rest --config /etc/
mongodb.conf --replSet $set_name --nojournal;
      fi
    fi
  end script
```

This task queue is simple. It consists of tasks that can be fired by a MongoDB. Anyone can write to the task queue, but only the master runs the tasks in the queue:

```
import os, utils, boto.sqs

# your amazon keys
key = os.environ['SQS_KEY_ID']
access = os.environ['SQS_ACCESS_KEY']
queue = os.environ['SQS_TASK_QUEUE']

if __name__ == '__main__':
    sqs = boto.sqs.connect_to_region(region,
                            aws_access_key_id = key,
                            aws_secret_access_key = access)

    tasks = sqs.create_queue(queue)
```

```
    # this is not really failsave. it would be better to check the return value
of
    # the mongo task, and only delete on successful execution.
    m = tasks.read()
    while m != None:
        body = m.get_body()
        os.system("/usr/bin/mongo --quiet --eval {0}".format(body))

        tasks.delete_message(m)

        m = tasks.read()
```

As you can see this is fairly rudimentary, but by choosing to work with services like SQS and SimpleDB we have not introduced another layer of infrastructure that we have to manage. Instead of making our application infrastructure more complex we made it simpler.

SNS

An alternative approach is to use SNS. You could send a message to an SNS topic, to be delivered to an SQS queue, and then be sent to some other place or mechanism (such as an event log).

Set endpoint

MongoDB's method of discovery is entirely handled by the client. Good client libraries only need to access the Replica Set through one of the members. The rest is automatic, more or less.

As with Postgres we use Route 53 to give nodes and clusters (Replica Sets) an end point. When we started this project Route 53 did not yet have weighted round robin DNS records. So we had to find another way.

We chose to have the master control the end point to the Replica Set. A master periodically (once every minute) checks the Route 53 record for the Replica Set. If it is does not point to itself, it changes it. (This happens when a new master is elected.) The Replica Set will continue to operate fine, except that the endpoint is not necessarily a valid entry point for a couple of minutes.

Master election

MongoDB has its internal master election process. This is convenient, because we don't have to consider race conditions or multiple masters.

Master election is notoriously difficult. You have to introduce notions of health and rules to deal with health changes. Two equally healthy nodes are eligible to assume the lead role, but we need another entity to make that decision. This is difficult to implement in general, but even more so without a central authority. If you deal with a software component that does not have this (like Postgres or Redis), you might have to choose a strategy and implement the tactics yourself.

These kinds of aspects make that distributed systems require very careful planning, execution, and relentless testing.

```python
# this script expects 2 environment variables
#       1. R53_KEY_ID (preferably an IAM user with limited rights)
#       2. R53_SECRET_KEY (accompanying secret key)
#       3. R53_TASK_QUEUE (the queue to use)

import os, platform

from boto.route53.connection import Route53Connection
from boto.route53.record import ResourceRecordSets

# your amazon keys
key = os.environ['R53_KEY_ID']
access = os.environ['R53_SECRET_KEY']

NAME = os.environ['SET_NAME']
HOSTED_ZONE_NAME = os.environ['HOSTED_ZONE_NAME']
HOSTED_ZONE_ID = os.environ['HOSTED_ZONE_ID']
hostname = platform.node()

if __name__ == '__main__':
    zones = {}
    value = ''
    route53 = Route53Connection(key, access)

    # get hosted zone for HOSTED_ZONE_NAME
    results = route53.get_hosted_zone(HOSTED_ZONE_ID)
    zone = results['GetHostedZoneResponse']['HostedZone']
    zone_id = zone['Id'].replace('/hostedzone/', '')
    zones[zone['Name']] = zone_id

    # first get the old value
    name = "{0}.{1}".format(NAME, HOSTED_ZONE_NAME)
    sets = route53.get_all_rrsets(zones[HOSTED_ZONE_NAME], None)
    for rset in sets:
        if rset.name == name:
            value = rset.resource_records[0]
```

```
# only change when necessary
if value != hostname:
    # first delete old record
    changes = ResourceRecordSets(route53, zone_id)

    if value != '':
        change = changes.add_change("DELETE", name, "CNAME", 60)
        change.add_value(value)

    # now, add ourselves as zuckerberg
    change = changes.add_change("CREATE", name, "CNAME", 60)
    change.add_value(platform.node())

    changes.commit()
```

Userdata

Joining (or initiating) a Replica Set requires the same userdata. If the Replica Set name exists, there are valid snapshots of an EBS volume with a version of the database, and those snapshots are used to bootstrap or join the set. The userdata for a Replica Set named mongodb, with 100GB storage space looks like this:

```
{
    "name"      :   "mongodb",
    "size"      :   100,
    "role"      :   "active"
}
```

To launch an arbiter in the same Replica Set:

```
{
    "name"      :   "mongodb",
    "role"      :   "arbiter"
}
```

In case you want to launch a Replica Set from a specific snapshot you can use the following userdata:

```
{
    "name"      :   "mongodb",
    "size"      :   100,
    "source"    :   "snap-78ee631b",
    "role"      :   "active"
}
```

Backups

With MongoDB 2.0 they introduced journaling. With journaling enabled it is easy to create a filesystem-based snapshot. Because we can easily (and quickly) make snapshots of our dbpath directory this is the obvious alternative.

When we started working on our solution there was no journaling yet, so we chose to use the lock/fsync/backup method. This is advertised for fast snapshots only, as writes are blocked. EBS snapshotting is fast enough.

Take regular snapshots

We can run this on a master, or a slave. For various reasons it is good to make regular, automated snapshots of your volumes.

Don't forget to implement snapshot purging. Snapshots also cost money.

To lock/fsync the database we run `/usr/bin/mongo --quiet admin /root/lock.js`, with `lock.js` like this:

```
#!/usr/bin/mongo admin

db.runCommand({fsync:1,lock:1});
db.currentOP();
```

To be absolutely sure we have a consistent snapshot we freeze (`xfs_freeze`) the mount point first.

Unlock is similar; we run `/usr/bin/mongo --quiet admin /root/unlock.js` with `unlock.js` like this:

```
#!/usr/bin/mongo admin

db.fsyncUnlock();
db.currentOP();
```

Shared resources

As with a database, a volume is a shared resource. If the volume is not unfrozen it is basically useless for other processes to work with. Your system grinds to a painful halt and it can be difficult to track down the source of the problem.

When implemented in Python a simple `try/finally` to make sure we don't leave frozen volumes. In bash, the absence of `try/finally` makes this more difficult.

Auto Scaling

Ultimately, you would like to have a self-healing Replica Set. If something goes wrong you will be alerted but only to supervise recovery. Like Postgres we will be pragmatic, but we can go a step further.

Remember that Postgres failover was fully manual. Because of this we didn't utilize AWS services like Auto Scaling, as it could get a bit too automated. But for MongoDB we can use Auto Scaling. If your components can be safely stopped and restarted, it does make sense to use Auto Scaling Groups of 1, to keep the replica set alive at all times.

We don't use Auto Scaling for growing or shrinking the Auto Scaling Group. We only use it to keep the group size intact. Setting up Auto Scaling for a typical MongoDB Replica Set looks like this:

```
$ userdata='{
        "name"          :   "mongodb",
        "size"          :   100,
        "role"          :   "active"
    }'

$ as-create-launch-config mongodb-9apps-net-lc-1 \
        --image-id ami-fd915694 \
        --instance-type m1.medium \
        --user-data "${userdata}" \
        --group mongodb

$ as-create-auto-scaling-group mongodb-9apps-net \
        --launch-configuration mongodb-9apps-net-lc-1 \
        --availability-zones eu-west-1a, eu-west-1b \
        --min-size 2 \
        --max-size 2

$ arbiter_userdata='{
        "name"          :   "mongodb",
        "role"          :   "arbiter"
    }'

$ as-create-launch-config arbiter-mongodb-9apps-net-lc-1 \
        --image-id ami-fd915694 \
        --instance-type t1.micro \
        --user-data "${arbiter_userdata}" \
        --group mongodb

$ as-create-auto-scaling-group arbiter-mongodb-9apps-net \
        --launch-configuration arbiter-mongodb-9apps-net-lc-1 \
        --availability-zones eu-west-1c \
        --min-size 1 \
        --max-size 1
```

It is now also easy to upgrade the Replica Set. All you need to do is change the Auto Scaling Group and rotate the instances. It is best to do this slowly, of course, as you don't want to lose the Replica Set.

```
$ userdata='{
        "name"          :   "mongodb",
        "size"          :   100,
        "role"          :   "active",
```

```
        }'

$ as-create-launch-config mongodb-9apps-net-lc-2 \
        --image-id ami-fd915695 \
        --instance-type m1.large \
        --user-data "${userdata}" \
        --group mongodb

$ as-update-auto-scaling-group mongodb-9apps-net \
        --launch-configuration mongodb-9apps-net-lc-2

$ as-terminate-instance-in-auto-scaling-group i-55f03d34 -D
$ as-terminate-instance-in-auto-scaling-group i-e16aaa80 -D

$ arbiter_userdata='{
        "name"          :   "mongodb",
        "role"          :   "arbiter"
    }'

$ as-create-launch-config arbiter-mongodb-9apps-net-lc-2 \
        --image-id ami-fd915695 \
        --instance-type t1.micro \
        --user-data "${arbiter_userdata}" \
        --group mongodb

$ as-update-auto-scaling-group arbiter-mongodb-9apps-net \
        --launch-configuration arbiter-mongodb-9apps-net-lc-2

$ as-terminate-instance-in-auto-scaling-group i-55f03d35 -D
```

Monitoring

We started this project quite a while back. At that time CloudWatch support in boto (the Python interface to AWS) was not 100% yet, so we used PHP to implement the monitoring.

For every member in the Replica Set we add metrics. The health of arbiters we get from the state of the Replica Set itself. We basically monitor every aspect MongoDB itself thinks is interesting enough to expose.

The Replica Set metrics are only added by the master. We particularly watch the UnHealthHostCount metric closely.

The full source of put-status.php:

```php
<?php

require_once 'AWSSDKforPHP/sdk.class.php';

define('AWS_KEY', getenv( 'EC2_KEY_ID'));
define('AWS_SECRET_KEY', getenv( 'EC2_SECRET_KEY'));
```

```php
define('AWS_ACCOUNT_ID', getenv( 'AWS_ACCOUNT_ID'));

$m = new Mongo();
$cw = new AmazonCloudWatch();
$cw->set_region('monitoring.' . getenv('EC2_REGION') . '.amazonaws.com');

$db = $m->admin;
$local = $m->selectDB( "local");

$replset = $local->selectCollection( "system.replset");
$replica_set_conf = $replset->findOne();

$ismaster = $db->command(array('ismaster'=>true));
$server_status = $db->command(array('serverStatus'=>true));
$replica_set_status =  $db->command(array('replSetGetStatus'=>true));

if( isset( $server_status['repl']['arbiterOnly']) && $server_status['repl']['ar-
biterOnly']) {
    $state = 'arbiter';
} else if( $server_status['repl']['ismaster']) {
    $state = 'primary';
} else {
    $state = 'secondary';
}

switch( $state) {
    case 'primary':
        # here we do the replica set metrics
        add_replica_set_metrics( $cw, $ismaster, $server_status,
                        $replica_set_status, $replica_set_conf);
    case 'secondary':
        # and the metrics for primary & secondary
        add_host_metrics( $cw, $ismaster, $server_status,
                        get_lag( $server_status['host'], $replica_set_status));
        break;
    case 'arbiter':
        # for an arbiter we don't add metrics, the health is
        # implicit in the replica set metrics
}

function add_replica_set_metrics( $cw, $ismaster, $server_status, $set_status,
$replica_set_conf) {
    $dimensions = array(
        array( 'Name' => 'ReplSet',
            'Value' => $server_status['repl']['setName'])
    );
    $timestamp = date( DATE_RFC822, $server_status['localTime']->sec);

    # set totals and assume all unhealthy
        $nr_hosts = $nr_unhealthy_hosts = count( $ismaster['hosts']);
        $nr_passives = $nr_unhealthy_passives =
                isset( $ismaster['passives']) && count( $ismaster['passives']) ?
```

```
                count( $ismaster['passives']) : 0;
        if( array_key_exists( 'arbiters', $ismaster)) {
            $nr_arbiters = $nr_unhealthy_arbiters =
                    count( $ismaster['arbiters']);
        } else {
            $nr_arbiters = $nr_unhealthy_arbiters = 0;
        }

        foreach( $set_status['members'] as $i => $member) {
        if( isset( $replica_set_conf['members'][$i]['priority']) &&
                $replica_set_conf['members'][$i]['priority'] == 0 ) {
            $nr_unhealthy_passives -= $member['health'];
        } else {
            if( $member['state'] == 1 or $member['state'] == 2) {
                # primary or secondary
                $nr_unhealthy_hosts -= $member['health'];
            } else if( $member['state'] == 7) {
                # arbiter
                $nr_unhealthy_arbiters -= $member['health'];
            }
        }
        }

    $metrics = array(
        array(
            'MetricName' => 'HealthyHostCount',
            'Dimensions' => $dimensions,
            'Value' => $nr_hosts - $nr_unhealthy_hosts,
            'Timestamp' => $timestamp,
            'Unit' => 'Count'
        ),
        array(
            'MetricName' => 'UnHealthyHostCount',
            'Dimensions' => $dimensions,
            'Value' => $nr_unhealthy_hosts,
            'Timestamp' => $timestamp,
            'Unit' => 'Count'
        ),
        array(
            'MetricName' => 'PassiveHostCount',
            'Dimensions' => $dimensions,
            'Value' => $nr_passives - $nr_unhealthy_passives,
            'Timestamp' => $timestamp,
            'Unit' => 'Count'
        ),
        array(
            'MetricName' => 'UnHealthyPassiveHostCount',
            'Dimensions' => $dimensions,
            'Value' => $nr_unhealthy_passives,
            'Timestamp' => $timestamp,
            'Unit' => 'Count'
        ),
```

```php
        array(
            'MetricName' => 'ArbiterCount',
            'Dimensions' => $dimensions,
            'Value' => $nr_arbiters - $nr_unhealthy_arbiters,
            'Timestamp' => $timestamp,
            'Unit' => 'Count'
        ),
        array(
            'MetricName' => 'UnHealthyArbiterCount',
            'Dimensions' => $dimensions,
            'Value' => $nr_unhealthy_arbiters,
            'Timestamp' => $timestamp,
            'Unit' => 'Count'
        )
    );

    $response = $cw->put_metric_data('9Apps/MongoDB', $metrics);
    if( !$response->isOK()) { print_r( $response); }
}

function add_host_metrics( $cw, $ismaster, $server_status, $lag) {
    $state = $ismaster['ismaster'] ? 'primary' : 'secondary';
    $timestamp = date( DATE_RFC822, $server_status['localTime']->sec);

    $replset = array( array(
        'Name' => 'ReplSet', 'Value' => $server_status['repl']['setName'])
    );

    $dimensions = array(
        array('Name' => 'Host', 'Value' => $server_status['host'])
    );

    # we can only add 20 metrics at most, so we need to do this twice
    $metrics = array(
        # first add the metric for aggregate
        array(
            'MetricName' => 'OperationsQueuedWaitingForLock',
            'Dimensions' => $replset,
            'Value' => $server_status['globalLock']['currentQueue']['total'],
            'Timestamp' => $timestamp,
            'Unit' => 'Count'
        ),
        # and don't forget the instance specific
        array(
            'MetricName' => 'OperationsQueuedWaitingForLock',
            'Dimensions' => $dimensions,
            'Value' => $server_status['globalLock']['currentQueue']['total'],
            'Timestamp' => $timestamp,
            'Unit' => 'Count'
        ),
        array(
            'MetricName' => 'ReadOperationsQueuedWaitingForLock',
```

```php
        'Dimensions' => $replset,
        'Value' => $server_status['globalLock']['currentQueue']['readers'],
        'Timestamp' => $timestamp,
        'Unit' => 'Count'
    ),
    array(
        'MetricName' => 'ReadOperationsQueuedWaitingForLock',
        'Dimensions' => $dimensions,
        'Value' => $server_status['globalLock']['currentQueue']['readers'],
        'Timestamp' => $timestamp,
        'Unit' => 'Count'
    ),
    array(
        'MetricName' => 'WriteOperationsQueuedWaitingForLock',
        'Dimensions' => $replset,
        'Value' => $server_status['globalLock']['currentQueue']['writers'],
        'Timestamp' => $timestamp,
        'Unit' => 'Count'
    ),
    array(
        'MetricName' => 'WriteOperationsQueuedWaitingForLock',
        'Dimensions' => $dimensions,
        'Value' => $server_status['globalLock']['currentQueue']['writers'],
        'Timestamp' => $timestamp,
        'Unit' => 'Count'
    ),
    array(
        'MetricName' => 'ActiveClients',
        'Dimensions' => $replset,
        'Value' => $server_status['globalLock']['activeClients']['total'],
        'Timestamp' => $timestamp,
        'Unit' => 'Count'
    ),
    array(
        'MetricName' => 'ActiveClients',
        'Dimensions' => $dimensions,
        'Value' => $server_status['globalLock']['activeClients']['total'],
        'Timestamp' => $timestamp,
        'Unit' => 'Count'
    ),
    array(
        'MetricName' => 'ActiveReaders',
        'Dimensions' => $replset,
        'Value' => $server_status['globalLock']['activeClients']['readers'],
        'Timestamp' => $timestamp,
        'Unit' => 'Count'
    ),
    array(
        'MetricName' => 'ActiveReaders',
        'Dimensions' => $dimensions,
        'Value' => $server_status['globalLock']['activeClients']['readers'],
        'Timestamp' => $timestamp,
```

```php
        'Unit' => 'Count'
    ),
    array(
        'MetricName' => 'ActiveWriters',
        'Dimensions' => $replset,
        'Value' => $server_status['globalLock']['activeClients']['writers'],
        'Timestamp' => $timestamp,
        'Unit' => 'Count'
    ),
    array(
        'MetricName' => 'ActiveWriters',
        'Dimensions' => $dimensions,
        'Value' => $server_status['globalLock']['activeClients']['writers'],
        'Timestamp' => $timestamp,
        'Unit' => 'Count'
    ),
    array(
        'MetricName' => 'ResidentMemory',
        'Dimensions' => $replset,
        'Value' => $server_status['mem']['resident'],
        'Timestamp' => $timestamp,
        'Unit' => 'Megabytes'
    ),
    array(
        'MetricName' => 'ResidentMemory',
        'Dimensions' => $dimensions,
        'Value' => $server_status['mem']['resident'],
        'Timestamp' => $timestamp,
        'Unit' => 'Megabytes'
    ),
    array(
        'MetricName' => 'VirtualMemory',
        'Dimensions' => $replset,
        'Value' => $server_status['mem']['virtual'],
        'Timestamp' => $timestamp,
        'Unit' => 'Megabytes'
    ),
    array(
        'MetricName' => 'VirtualMemory',
        'Dimensions' => $dimensions,
        'Value' => $server_status['mem']['virtual'],
        'Timestamp' => $timestamp,
        'Unit' => 'Megabytes'
    ),
    array(
        'MetricName' => 'MappedMemory',
        'Dimensions' => $replset,
        'Value' => $server_status['mem']['mapped'],
        'Timestamp' => $timestamp,
        'Unit' => 'Megabytes'
    ),
    array(
```

```php
            'MetricName' => 'MappedMemory',
            'Dimensions' => $dimensions,
            'Value' => $server_status['mem']['mapped'],
            'Timestamp' => $timestamp,
            'Unit' => 'Megabytes'
        ),
        array(
            'MetricName' => 'ActiveConnections',
            'Dimensions' => $replset,
            'Value' => $server_status['connections']['current'],
            'Timestamp' => $timestamp,
            'Unit' => 'Count'
        ),
        array(
            'MetricName' => 'ActiveConnections',
            'Dimensions' => $dimensions,
            'Value' => $server_status['connections']['current'],
            'Timestamp' => $timestamp,
            'Unit' => 'Count'
        ),
    ));
    $response = $cw->put_metric_data('9Apps/MongoDB', $metrics);
    if( !$response->isOK()) { print_r( $response); }

    $metrics = array(
        array(
            'MetricName' => 'LastFlushOperation',
            'Dimensions' => $replset,
            'Value' => $server_status['backgroundFlushing']['last_ms'],
            'Timestamp' => $timestamp,
            'Unit' => 'Milliseconds'
        ),
        array(
            'MetricName' => 'LastFlushOperation',
            'Dimensions' => $dimensions,
            'Value' => $server_status['backgroundFlushing']['last_ms'],
            'Timestamp' => $timestamp,
            'Unit' => 'Milliseconds'
        ),
        array(
            'MetricName' => 'OpenCursors',
            'Dimensions' => $replset,
            'Value' => $server_status['cursors']['totalOpen'],
            'Timestamp' => $timestamp,
            'Unit' => 'Count'
        ),
        array(
            'MetricName' => 'OpenCursors',
            'Dimensions' => $dimensions,
            'Value' => $server_status['cursors']['totalOpen'],
            'Timestamp' => $timestamp,
            'Unit' => 'Count'
        ),
```

```php
    );

    # add lag if secondary
    if( !$ismaster['ismaster']) {
        $metrics[] = array(
                'MetricName' => 'Lag',
                'Dimensions' => $dimensions,
                'Value' => $lag,
                'Timestamp' => $timestamp,
                'Unit' => 'Seconds'
        );
    }
    $response = $cw->put_metric_data('9Apps/MongoDB', $metrics);
    if( !$response->isOK()) { print_r( $response); }
}

# return lag of host, relative to master
function get_lag( $host, $replica_set_status) {
    foreach( $replica_set_status['members'] as $member) {
        if( $member['state'] == 1) {
            $base = $member['optime']->sec;
        }

        if( strpos( $member['name'], $host) !== false) {
            $me = $member['optime']->sec;
        }

        # we are done when we are done
        if( isset( $base) && isset( $me)) break;
    }

    return $me - $base;
}

?>
```

Conclusion

We have been running MongoDB this way for several years now—it has survived several AWS glitches, with no data loss, and we have restored full Replica Sets several times.

This project is a bit older, but we still run it like this. If we were to build it now, we would build it solely using one software platform, probably boto/Python. And we would use a couple of different techniques Amazon AWS has to offer, like weighted round robin DNS records.

But, MongoDB has served us well, and we do not see the need to make these changes at this moment.

## CHAPTER 8

Redis

Redis is an open source, advanced key-value store. It is often referred to as a data structure server since keys can contain strings, hashes, lists, sets, and sorted sets.

Redis (*http://redis.io*) has a very novel approach to being a datastore. Actually, its own *data structure server* is a very apt description: it is a server.

As with all our infrastructure components, we aim for resilience (does not break easily) and reliability (does what you expect it to do). For Redis, we have to figure out how to do the following:

- Backup/restore
- Failover
- Scaling (up and down)
- Monitoring

This project is available on github at ReDiS (*https://github.com/9apps/redis*).

The Problem

Redis as a data structure server finds its limits in *the server*. The core idea is that it exposes the memory on an instance as a variety of structured data through an API. This is fast but very fragile. Memory is not persisted.

This feature has two consequences we have to deal with:

1. Persistence (how to make backups)
2. Replication

Both these problems would go away if Redis were available in a distributed manner. In the next chapter, we'll see how elasticsearch elegantly solves this shortcoming. But the distributed Redis is a work in progress and we don't know when it will be available. In the meantime, we have our own workaround.

Our Approach

Redis has the notion of master-slave replication. In Redis anything can be a master, and masters are almost completely unaware of existing slaves. A slave has only one master, which is slaveof.

This simple approach to replication is very powerful, and we'll use it to our advantage. To solve replication (and a bit of horizontal scalability), we'll chain Redis into resilience.

Our Redis chain is a unidirectional linked list. It has a head, a tail (perhaps the same), and perhaps nodes in between. The nature of this list is that every slave is behind its master.

If a node dies for whatever reason, its slave (if there is one) has to re-slave itself to the master of its previous master, or become a master itself. *How?* you might ask. The answer is: if we have slaves that can automatically look for a new master, the chain will heal itself.

The head is for writing only, but the slaves can also be used for reading.

Implementation

This project is again nearly 100% boto/Python. With the excellent Python redis client (pip install redis) we can do everything we want. Our install looks like this:

```
# check http://redis.io/download for the latest
$ wget http://redis.googlecode.com/files/redis-2.4.5.tar.gz
$ tar xzvf redis-2.4.5.tar.gz
$ cd redis-2.4.5
$ make
$ apt-get install tcl8.5
$ make test
$ make install

$ adduser --disabled-password --no-create-home --gecos "Redis Server" redis

$ cat <<EOF > /etc/logrotate.d/redis
/var/log/redis/*.log {
        daily
        rotate 14
        copytruncate
        delaycompress
        compress
```

```
        notifempty
        missingok
}
EOF

# install redis.py (the 'official' python redis client)
$ pip install redis
```

Apart from this, we install the EC2 command-line tools, because we can't designate a volume to be deleted upon termination with boto.

We'll also create an IAM user with more or less the same privileges as we saw in the previous chapters on Postgres and MongoDB.

userdata

```
{
    "name"             :   "kate",
    "persistence"      :   "normal",
    "monitoring"       :   "on",
    "maxmemory"        :   "on",
    "maxmemory-policy" :   "noeviction",
    "logging"          :   "warning"
}
```

We want to dictate a Redis instance/chain by userdata. Depending on your requirements we can launch it with a certain level of persistence. Default is *normal*.

no
> No snapshots, no dumps, nothing

low
> Dumps to S3 (RDB) and EBS snapshots

normal
> Low + AOF (append only file, with default configuration)

high
> Normal + AOF is append always (every change is appended)

The default logging is *warning*. You can change that to *error*, if you want less. Or to *info*, if you want to see all. Events are logged in SimpleDB. Default is unset, meaning no logging at all.

The monitoring parameter can be set to (default is *off*).

off
> No CloudWatch monitoring

on
> CloudWatch monitoring of Redis system state

all

    Monitoring of system state and *size* of all keys present

The parameter `maxmemory` needs some explanation. If you are using your system as a database, you never want the system to start getting rid of keys *randomly*. But if you are using your system for caching, then it does make sense. If used as cache, memcached should be discarded first. For `maxmemory`, *on* means we'll set the max to 60% of available system memory. By default this is *off*.

With the maxmemory policy, you can override the default eviction policy. The value you give here will be copied verbatim to the config, there is no checking for validity. The default for `maxmemory-policy` is empty in case `maxmemory` is not off, using the default of Redis (which may change over time).

Redis

As by now you might have realized, we like the default settings in Redis. Everything that you change adds complexity and for every change you need a very good reason.

Let start with our `init.d`, our start/stop script:

```sh
#! /bin/sh
### BEGIN INIT INFO
# Provides: redis-server
# Required-Start:    $syslog
# Required-Stop:     $syslog
# Default-Start:     2 3 4 5
# Default-Stop:      0 1 6
# Short-Description: redis-server - Persistent key-value db
# Description: redis-server - Persistent key-value db
### END INIT INFO


PATH=/usr/local/sbin:/usr/local/bin:/sbin:/bin:/usr/sbin:/usr/bin
DAEMON=/usr/local/bin/redis-server
DAEMON_ARGS=/etc/redis/redis.conf
NAME=redis-server
DESC=redis-server
PIDFILE=/var/run/redis/redis.pid

test -x $DAEMON || exit 0
test -x $DAEMONBOOTSTRAP || exit 0

set -e

case "$1" in
  start)
    echo -n "Starting $DESC: "

    mkdir -p /var/lib/redis
```

```
    chown redis.redis /var/lib/redis

    mkdir -p /var/log/redis
    chown redis.redis /var/log/redis

    mkdir -p /var/run/redis
    chown redis.redis /var/run/redis

    # prepare for running redis
    /root/ReDiS/prepare.sh

    if start-stop-daemon --start --quiet --umask 007 \
            --pidfile $PIDFILE --user redis --group redis \
            --exec $DAEMON -- $DAEMON_ARGS
    then
      echo "$NAME."

      # now, 'join' the cluster
      /root/ReDiS/join.sh
    else
     echo "failed"
    fi
  ;;
  stop)
    echo -n "Stopping $DESC: "

    # first, 'leave' the cluster
    /root/ReDiS/leave.sh
    if start-stop-daemon --stop --retry 10 --quiet --oknodo
            --pidfile $PIDFILE --exec $DAEMON
    then
      echo "$NAME."
      # and now, decommission
      /root/ReDiS/decommission.sh
    else
      echo "failed"
    fi
  ;;
  restart|force-reload)
    ${0} stop
    ${0} start
    ;;
  *)
    echo "Usage: /etc/init.d/$NAME {start|stop|restart|force-reload}" >&2
    exit 1
  ;;
esac

exit 0
```

prepare.sh/prepare.py deal with getting the instance ready to do work. Most of these scripts deal with persistence (see below) but there is one part we want to mention here.

Configuration (maxmemory)

Redis is pretty volatile. If you do not treat it gently, it might blow up in your face. Because not all applications play nicely with their environments we introduced maxmemory settings. This is basically a failsafe option to protect data, something you would like the application to take responsibility for.

```
dst = "/etc/redis/redis.conf"
redis = "{0}/etc/redis/{1}.conf".format(path, persistence)
cron = "{0}/cron.d/{1}.cron".format(path, persistence)

# redis will start with this conf
log('configuring redis', 'info')
os.system("/bin/cp -f {0} {1}".format(redis, dst))
if maxmemory > 0:
        os.system("/bin/sed 's/^# maxmemory <bytes>.*$/maxmemory {0}/' -i
{1}".format(maxmemory, dst))

    if policy != None:
            os.system("/bin/sed 's/^# maxmemory-policy.*$/maxmemory-policy
{0}/' -i {1}".format(policy,dst))
```

The Redis configuration files are dependent on the persistence level, which are taken from the Redis install directory. maxmemory and policy are read from userdata.

Persistence

In Redis, there are several ways to achieve persistence. You have RDB (point in time database snapshots) and AOF (append-only file). So, we can use full database dumps (RDB) or rely on replaying the logfile (AOF) for re-creating a database. However, we also have a third way: EBS snapshots.

We can configure our Redis instance to create RDB dumps and copy them to S3. We can also tell Redis to write the AOF in several different ways. The default way is every sec, which is fine for most apps. But you can set it to always, in which case all changes are persisted to AOF. This is also the most costly way. The default way of everysec is fine for most applications.

```
# Copyright (C) 2011, 2012 9apps B.V.
#
# This file is part of Redis for AWS.
#
# Redis for AWS is free software: you can redistribute it and/or modify
# it under the terms of the GNU General Public License as published by
# the Free Software Foundation, either version 3 of the License, or
# (at your option) any later version.
#
# Redis for AWS is distributed in the hope that it will be useful,
# but WITHOUT ANY WARRANTY; without even the implied warranty of
# MERCHANTABILITY or FITNESS FOR A PARTICULAR PURPOSE.  See the
# GNU General Public License for more details.
```

```
#
# You should have received a copy of the GNU General Public License
# along with Redis for AWS. If not, see <http://www.gnu.org/licenses/>.

import os, sys, re, json

from boto.ec2.connection import EC2Connection
from boto.ec2.regioninfo import RegionInfo

import backup, administration
from events import Events
from host import Host

# Ubuntu 12.04 uses recent kernels (/dev/xvdf), EC2 not yet (/dev/sdf)
def DEVICE(device):
    return device.replace('/s', '/xv')

self.userdata = json.loads(boto.utils.get_instance_userdata())
self.metadata = boto.utils.get_instance_metadata()

instance_id = self.metadata['instance-id']
hostname = self.metadata['public-hostname']
zone = self.metadata['placement']['availability-zone']
region = zone[:-1]

device = "/dev/sdf"
mount = "/var/lib/redis"

# what is the domain to work with
redis_name = os.environ['REDIS_NAME'].strip()
hosted_zone = os.environ['HOSTED_ZONE_NAME'].rstrip('.')

# the name (and identity) of the cluster (the master)
cluster = "{0}.{1}".format(redis_name, hosted_zone)

events = Events(sys.argv[1], sys.argv[2], cluster)
node = Host(cluster, events).get_node()
component = os.path.basename(sys.argv[0])
def log(message, logging='warning'):
    events.log(node, component, message, logging)

# we are going to work with local files, we need our path
path = os.path.dirname(os.path.abspath(__file__))

def provision(key, access, cluster, size, maxmemory=-1, policy=None, persis-
tence="no", snapshot=None, rdb=None):
    log('start provisioning', 'info')
    # ec2 is region specific
    ec2 = boto.ec2.connect_to_region(region,
                          aws_access_key_id = key,
                          aws_secret_access_key = access)
```

```python
def add_monitor(device="/dev/sdf", name="main"):
    f = open( "{0}/etc/monit/{1}".format(path, name), "w")
    f.write("  check filesystem {0} with path {1}".format(name,
                            DEVICE(device)))
    f.write("   if failed permission 660 then alert")
    f.write("   if failed uid root then alert")
    f.write("   if failed gid disk then alert")
      f.write("    if space usage > 80% for 5 times within 15 cycles then
alert")
    f.close()

def create_device(snapshot=None):
    log('getting a device', 'info')
    # if we have the device (/dev/sdf) just don't do anything anymore
    mapping = ec2.get_instance_attribute(instance_id, 'blockDeviceMapping')
    try:
        volume_id = mapping['blockDeviceMapping'][DEVICE(device)].volume_id
        log('using existing volume', 'info')
    except:
        log('creating a new volume', 'info')
        volume = ec2.create_volume(size, zone, snapshot)
        volume.attach(instance_id, DEVICE(device))
        volume_id = volume.id
        log('created ' + volume_id, 'info')

        # we can't continue without a properly attached device
        log('waiting for ' + DEVICE(device), 'info')
            os.system("while [ ! -b {0} ] ; do /bin/true ; done".format(DE-
VICE(device)))

        # make sure the volume is deleted upon termination
        # should also protect from disaster like loosing an instance
        # (it doesn't work with boto, so we do it 'outside')
        log('set delete-on-termination', 'info')
            os.system("/usr/bin/ec2-modify-instance-attribute --block-device-
mapping \"{0}=:true\" {1} --region {2}".format(DEVICE(device), instance_id, re-
gion))

        # if we start from snapshot we are almost done
        if snapshot == "" or None == snapshot:
            log('creating a filesystem', 'info')
            # first create filesystem
            os.system("/sbin/mkfs.xfs {0}".format(DEVICE(device)))

        log('mounting the filesystem', 'info')
        log('(but cleaning the mountpoint first)', 'info')
        os.system("/bin/rm -rf {0}/*".format(mount))
        # mount, but first wait until the device is ready
          os.system("/bin/mount -t xfs -o defaults {0} {1}".format(DEVICE(de-
vice), mount))
        # and grow (if necessary)
```

```
        log('growing the filesystem', 'info')
        os.system("/usr/sbin/xfs_growfs {0}".format(mount))

        add_monitor(DEVICE(device), 'data')

        log('volume {0} is attached to {1} and mounted ({2}) and ready for
use'.format(volume_id, DEVICE(device), mount), 'info')
        return volume_id

    def prepare():
        log('prepare the environment', 'info')
        # from this point we are sure we don't have to be careful
        # with local files/devices/disks/etc

        dst = "/etc/redis/redis.conf"
        redis = "{0}/etc/redis/{1}.conf".format(path, persistence)
        cron = "{0}/cron.d/{1}.cron".format(path, persistence)

        # redis will start with this conf
        log('configuring redis', 'info')
        os.system("/bin/cp -f {0} {1}".format(redis, dst))
        if maxmemory > 0:
            os.system("/bin/sed 's/^# maxmemory <bytes>.*$/maxmemory {0}/' -i
{1}".format(maxmemory, dst))

            if policy != None:
                os.system("/bin/sed 's/^# maxmemory-policy.*$/maxmemory-policy
{0}/' -i {1}".format(policy, dst))

        # and root's cron will be set accordingly as well
        log('setting up cron', 'info')
            os.system("/bin/sed  's:INSTALLPATH:{0}:'  {1}  |  /usr/bin/cron-
tab".format(path, cron))

        # ok, ready to set up assets like bucket and volume
        # also, if we have a valid mount, we don't do anything
        log('set up persistence', 'info')
        if os.path.ismount(mount) == False and "no" != persistence:
            log('create bucket {0}'.format(cluster), 'info')
            backup.create_bucket(key, access, cluster)

            try:
                # only try to create one if we have one
                if "" == snapshot or None == snapshot:
                    raise Exception('metadata','empty snapshot')
                else:
                    create_device(snapshot)
            except:
                try:
                    latest = administration.get_latest_snapshot(key,

                    access, cluster)
```

```
                    create_device(latest)
                except:
                    create_device()

            # we have a bucket, and perhaps a device. lets try to restore
            # from rdb, first from metadata later from user_data.
            if rdb != None and "" != rdb:
                log('restore rdb {0}/{1}'.format(cluster, rdb), 'info')
                backup.restore(key, access, cluster, rdb)

            latest = administration.get_latest_RDB(key, access, cluster)
            if "" != latest and None != latest:
                log('restore rdb {0}/{1}'.format(cluster, latest), 'info')
                backup.restore(key, access, cluster, latest)

    prepare()

def meminfo():
    """
    dict of data from meminfo (str:int).
    Values are in kilobytes.
    """
    re_parser = re.compile(r'^(?P<key>\S*):\s*(?P<value>\d*)\s*kB')
    result = dict()
    for line in open('/proc/meminfo'):
        match = re_parser.match(line)
        if not match:
            continue # skip lines that don't parse
        key, value = match.groups(['key', 'value'])
        result[key] = int(value)
    return result

if __name__ == '__main__':
    import os, sys

    try:
        persistence = userdata['persistence']
    except:
        persistence = None
    try:
        snapshot = userdata['snapshot']
    except:
        snapshot = None
    try:
        rdb = userdata['rdb']
    except:
        rdb = None

    maxmemory = -1
    policy = None
    try:
        if userdata['maxmemory'] == 'on':
```

```
        maxmemory = int(0.8 * (meminfo()['MemTotal'] * 1024))

    try:
        policy = userdata['maxmemory-policy']
    except:
        pass
    except:
        pass

    size = 3 * ( meminfo()['MemTotal'] / ( 1024 * 1024 ) )
    # set a default size of 5 gigs just incase we are using a micro instance.
    # Usefult for playing around with this project
    size = 5 if size == 0 else size

    provision(sys.argv[1], sys.argv[2], cluster, size, maxmemory, policy,
                          persistence=persistence, snapshot=snapshot,
rdb=rdb)
```

In our experience, Redis persistence is quite problematic. In high traffic environments both RDB and AOF incur serious performance penalties. We mostly rely on replication (see below) for durability of the data.

The new IOPS EBS volumes might bring some relief to IO traffic incurred through RDB operations and writing to the AOF, in that we can use it for replication of our data. Perhaps even SSD can help overcome this. But in our opinion this is to be solved in the software itself. Persistence, at this moment, is an afterthought to the core concept of Redis, which is an *in-memory datastore*.

Monitoring

As we did with MongoDB and Postgres, we'll use CloudWatch for monitoring our Redis system. For Redis we want to switch monitoring on and off (because it is not always necessary for development or test environments). But we also want to do a little bit more.

Sometimes Redis is used for queue style data. In this case, we would like to monitor the size of the keys in Redis. This is not always feasible, as you can end up with thousands of metrics. Apart from the cost (which is pretty significant) it also renders the Cloud-Watch part of the AWS Console useless for practical purposes.

Here is the monitoring script:

```
# Copyright (C) 2011, 2012 9apps B.V.
#
# This file is part of Redis for AWS.
#
# Redis for AWS is free software: you can redistribute it and/or modify
# it under the terms of the GNU General Public License as published by
# the Free Software Foundation, either version 3 of the License, or
# (at your option) any later version.
#
# Redis for AWS is distributed in the hope that it will be useful,
```

```
# but WITHOUT ANY WARRANTY; without even the implied warranty of
# MERCHANTABILITY or FITNESS FOR A PARTICULAR PURPOSE.  See the
# GNU General Public License for more details.
#
# You should have received a copy of the GNU General Public License
# along with Redis for AWS. If not, see <http://www.gnu.org/licenses/>.


import os, sys, redis, json, hashlib

from datetime import datetime

import boto.utils, boto.ec2.cloudwatch

#
# REDIS MONITOR
#
#
class Monitor:
    def __init__(self, key, access, cluster):
        self.userdata = json.loads(boto.utils.get_instance_userdata())
        self.metadata = boto.utils.get_instance_metadata()

        public_hostname = self.metadata['public-hostname']
        zone = self.metadata['placement']['availability-zone']
        region = zone[:-1]

        # the name (and identity) of the cluster (the master)
        self.cluster = cluster

        self.redis = redis.StrictRedis(host='localhost', port=6379)

        self.cloudwatch = boto.ec2.cloudwatch.connect_to_region(region,
                        aws_access_key_id = key,
                        aws_secret_access_key = access)
        self.namespace = '9apps/redis'

        # get the host, but without the logging
        self.node = public_hostname

    def collect(self, monitoring = 'on'):
        if monitoring not in ['on', 'all']:
            return [[], [], [], {}]

        now = datetime.utcnow()

        items = self.redis.info()

        names = []
        values = []
        units = []
        dimensions = { 'node' : self.node,
```

```
                          'cluster' : self.cluster }

slowlog_len = self.redis.execute_command('SLOWLOG','LEN')
names.append('slowlog_len')
values.append(slowlog_len)
units.append('Count')

if items['aof_enabled']:
    names.append('bgrewriteaof_in_progress')
    values.append(items['bgrewriteaof_in_progress'])
    units.append('Count')

    names.append('aof_pending_bio_fsync')
    values.append(items['aof_pending_bio_fsync'])
    units.append('Count')

    names.append('aof_buffer_length')
    values.append(items['aof_buffer_length'])
    units.append('Count')

    names.append('aof_current_size')
    values.append(items['aof_current_size'])
    units.append('Bytes')

    names.append('aof_pending_rewrite')
    values.append(items['aof_pending_rewrite'])
    units.append('Count')

    names.append('aof_base_size')
    values.append(items['aof_base_size'])
    units.append('Bytes')

# master/slave
names.append(items['role'])
values.append(1)
units.append('Count')

for item in items:
    if item >= 'db0' and item < 'dc':
        names.append("{0}_keys".format(item))
        values.append(items[item]['keys'])
        units.append('Count')

        names.append("{0}_expires".format(item))
        values.append(items[item]['expires'])
        units.append('Count')

        # and now add some info on the keys, if we want
        if monitoring == 'all':
            nr = item.lstrip('db')
            db = redis.StrictRedis(host='localhost', port=6379, db=nr)
            keys = db.keys('*')
```

```
                for key in keys:
                    key_type = db.type(key)
                    key = key.replace( '.', '_')

                    if key_type == "list":
                        llen = db.llen(key)
                        names.append("{0}_{1}_llen".format(item, key))
                        values.append(llen)
                        units.append('Count')
                    elif key_type == "hash":
                        hlen = db.hlen(key)
                        names.append("{0}_{1}_hlen".format(item, key))
                        values.append(hlen)
                        units.append('Count')
                    elif key_type == "set":
                        scard = db.scard(key)
                        names.append("{0}_{1}_scard".format(item, key))
                        values.append(scard)
                        units.append('Count')
                    elif key_type == "zset":
                        zcard = db.zcard(key)
                        names.append("{0}_{1}_zcard".format(item, key))
                        values.append(zcard)
                        units.append('Count')
                    elif key_type == "string":
                        strlen = db.strlen(key)
                        names.append("{0}_{1}_strlen".format(item, key))
                        values.append(strlen)
                        units.append('Count')

        # pub/sub
        names.append('pubsub_channels')
        values.append(items['pubsub_channels'])
        units.append('Count')

        names.append('pubsub_patterns')
        values.append(items['pubsub_patterns'])
        units.append('Count')

        # memory
        names.append('used_memory')
        values.append(items['used_memory'])
        units.append('Bytes')

        names.append('used_memory_peak')
        values.append(items['used_memory_peak'])
        units.append('Bytes')

        names.append('used_memory_rss')
        values.append(items['used_memory_rss'])
        units.append('Bytes')
```

```
names.append('mem_fragmentation_ratio')
values.append(items['mem_fragmentation_ratio'])
units.append('None')

names.append('connected_slaves')
values.append(items['connected_slaves'])
units.append('Count')

#
names.append('loading')
values.append(items['loading'])
units.append('Count')

names.append('bgsave_in_progress')
values.append(items['bgsave_in_progress'])
units.append('Count')

# clients
names.append('connected_clients')
values.append(items['connected_clients'])
units.append('Count')

names.append('blocked_clients')
values.append(items['blocked_clients'])
units.append('Count')

# connection/command totals
#names.append('total_connections_received')
#values.append(items['total_connections_received'])
#units.append('Count')

#names.append('total_commands_processed')
#values.append(items['total_commands_processed'])
#units.append('Count')

# client input/output
names.append('client_biggest_input_buf')
values.append(items['client_biggest_input_buf'])
units.append('Bytes')

names.append('client_longest_output_list')
values.append(items['client_longest_output_list'])
units.append('Bytes')

# keys
names.append('expired_keys')
values.append(items['expired_keys'])
units.append('Count')

names.append('evicted_keys')
values.append(items['evicted_keys'])
units.append('Count')
```

```python
        # last_save
        names.append('changes_since_last_save')
        values.append(items['changes_since_last_save'])
        units.append('Count')

        # keyspace
        #names.append('keyspace_misses')
        #values.append(items['keyspace_misses'])
        #units.append('Count')

        #names.append('keyspace_hits')
        #values.append(items['keyspace_hits'])
        #units.append('Count')

        return [names, values, units, dimensions]

    def put(self):
        result = False
        try:
            # only monitor if we are told to (this will break, if not set)
            monitoring = self.userdata['monitoring']
        except:
            monitoring = 'on'

        if monitoring in ['on', 'all']:
            # first get all we need
            [names, values, units, dimensions] = self.collect(monitoring)
            print [names, values, units, dimensions]
            while len(names) > 0:
                names20 = names[:20]
                values20 = values[:20]
                units20 = units[:20]

                # we can't send all at once, only 20 at a time
                # first aggregated over all
                result = self.cloudwatch.put_metric_data(self.namespace,
                                                  names20, value=values20,
unit=units20)
                for dimension in dimensions:
                    dimension = { dimension : dimensions[dimension] }
                    result &= self.cloudwatch.put_metric_data(
                                            self.namespace, names20, value=val-
ues20,
                                            unit=units20, dimensions=dimension)

                del names[:20]
                del values[:20]
                del units[:20]
        else:
            print "we are not monitoring"
```

```
        return result

    def metrics(self):
        return self.cloudwatch.list_metrics()

if __name__ == '__main__':
    key = os.environ['EC2_KEY_ID']
    access = os.environ['EC2_SECRET_KEY']

    name = os.environ['REDIS_NAME'].strip()
    zone = os.environ['HOSTED_ZONE_NAME'].rstrip('.')
    cluster = "{0}.{1}".format(name, zone)

    # easy testing, use like this (requires environment variables)
    #       python cluster.py get_master cluster 2c922342a.cluster
    monitor = Monitor(key, access, cluster)
    print getattr(monitor, sys.argv[1])(*sys.argv[3:])
```

As you can see, this is more or less the same as the other monitoring scripts. But because we could end up with hundreds of metrics we have to add them in groups of 20. (Even with hundreds of keys running this every minute does not cause performance problems.)

Chaining (Replication)

Now that we have a properly running Redis, it is time to put it into context. Lets create chains of Redis instances.

Again, we designed this component to function without *central oversight*. We do not want to introduce yet another server that can fail.

We do, however, need *central administration*. For this we turn to SimpleDB and Route 53. We will use SimpleDB to administer the chain, and Route 53 to identify the different parts of the chain.

Lets start with join.py, which is called right after the Redis daemon is launched:

```
# Copyright (C) 2011, 2012 9apps B.V.
#
# This file is part of Redis for AWS.
#
# Redis for AWS is free software: you can redistribute it and/or modify
# it under the terms of the GNU General Public License as published by
# the Free Software Foundation, either version 3 of the License, or
# (at your option) any later version.
#
# Redis for AWS is distributed in the hope that it will be useful,
# but WITHOUT ANY WARRANTY; without even the implied warranty of
# MERCHANTABILITY or FITNESS FOR A PARTICULAR PURPOSE.  See the
# GNU General Public License for more details.
#
# You should have received a copy of the GNU General Public License
```

```
# along with Redis for AWS. If not, see <http://www.gnu.org/licenses/>.

import os, sys, json

from cluster import Cluster
from host import Host
from route53 import Route53Zone

from events import Events

# your amazon keys
key = os.environ['EC2_KEY_ID']
access = os.environ['EC2_SECRET_KEY']

# what is the domain to work with
name = os.environ['REDIS_NAME'].strip()
zone_name = os.environ['HOSTED_ZONE_NAME']
zone_id = os.environ['HOSTED_ZONE_ID']

# the name (and identity) of the cluster (the master)
cluster = "{0}.{1}".format(name, zone_name.rstrip('.'))

# get/create the cluster environment
cluster = Cluster(key, access, cluster)
r53_zone = Route53Zone(key, access, zone_id)
ec2 = EC2(key, access)

events = Events(key, access, cluster.name())
host = Host(cluster.name(), events)
node = host.get_node()
endpoint = host.get_endpoint()
component = os.path.basename(sys.argv[0])
def log(message, logging='info'):
    events.log(node, component, message, logging)

if __name__ == '__main__':
    log('joining the cluster', 'info')

    log('adding the node to the cluster', 'info')
    # now we are ready to be (added to) the cluster
    cluster.add_node(node, endpoint)
    log('creating a Route53 records', 'info')
    r53_zone.create_record(node, endpoint)
    log('setting the tag', 'info')
    ec2.set_tag(node)

    log('getting the master of the node', 'info')
    master = cluster.get_master(node)
    # if we don't have a master, we ARE the master
    if master == None:
        log('setting the main Route53 record for the cluster', 'info')
        r53_zone.update_record(cluster.name(), endpoint)
```

```
        # and make sure we 'run' correctly (no-slave, well-monitored)
        log('set the host to run as master', 'info')
        host.set_master()
    else:
        # attach to the master (and start watching its availability)
        log('set the host to run as slave of {0}'.format(master), 'info')
        host.set_master(master)

    log('joined the cluster', 'info')
```

join.py organizes the joining process; the actual slaving is done in host.py:

```
# Copyright (C) 2011, 2012 9apps B.V.
#
# This file is part of Redis for AWS.
#
# Redis for AWS is free software: you can redistribute it and/or modify
# it under the terms of the GNU General Public License as published by
# the Free Software Foundation, either version 3 of the License, or
# (at your option) any later version.
#
# Redis for AWS is distributed in the hope that it will be useful,
# but WITHOUT ANY WARRANTY; without even the implied warranty of
# MERCHANTABILITY or FITNESS FOR A PARTICULAR PURPOSE.  See the
# GNU General Public License for more details.
#
# You should have received a copy of the GNU General Public License
# along with Redis for AWS. If not, see <http://www.gnu.org/licenses/>.


import os, sys, time, json, hashlib
import boto.utils, redis

from events import Events


#
# REDIS HOST
#
# ...
#
class Host:
    def __init__(self, cluster, events=None):
        self.endpoint = boto.utils.get_instance_metadata()['public-hostname']
        self.userdata = json.loads(boto.utils.get_instance_userdata())

        self.cluster = cluster
        self.id = hashlib.md5(self.endpoint).hexdigest()[:8]
        self.node = "{0}.{1}".format(self.id, self.cluster)
        self.master = None

        self.redis = redis.StrictRedis(host="localhost", port=6379)
        self.events = events
```

```python
    def __log(self, message, logging='warning'):
        try:
            self.events.log(self.node, 'Host', message, logging)
        except:
            print "probably no 'events' object supplied"

    def get_node(self):
        self.__log('get_node', 'info')
        return self.node

    def get_endpoint(self):
        self.__log('get_endpoint', 'info')
        return self.endpoint

    def get_master(self):
        self.__log('get_master', 'info')
        return self.master

    def set_master(self, master=None):
        self.__log('set_master: {0}'.format(master), 'info')
        self.master = master
        try:
            os.system("/usr/bin/monit monitor redis")
            if None == master:
                try:
                    self.__log('slaveof()', 'info')
                    self.redis.slaveof()
                finally:
                    self.__log('monit unmonitor initializing', 'info')
                    os.system("/usr/bin/monit unmonitor initializing")

                    self.__log('monit unmonitor slave', 'info')
                    os.system("/usr/bin/monit unmonitor slave")
            else:
                try:
                    self.__log('slaveof({0})'.format(master), 'info')
                    while True:
                        try:
                            self.redis.slaveof(master, 6379)
                                self.__log('master now: ({0})'.format(master),
'info')
                            break
                        except Exception as e:
                            self.__log(e, 'error')
                            if str(e) == "Redis is loading data into memory":
                                self.__log('retrying slaveof, in a sec', 'info')
                                time.sleep(1)
                            else:
                                self.__log('different error', 'info')
                                raise e
                finally:
```

```
                    self.__log('monit monitor initializing', 'info')
                    os.system("/usr/bin/monit monitor initializing")

                    self.__log('monit monitor slave', 'info')
                    os.system("/usr/bin/monit monitor slave")
            except Exception as e:
                self.__log(e, 'error')

    if __name__ == '__main__':
        # easy testing, use like this (requires environment variables)
        #       python host.py set_master cluster 2c922342a.cluster
        host = Host(sys.argv[2])
        print getattr(host, sys.argv[1])(*sys.argv[3:])
```

The state of Redis is important. With bigger data sets we have to patiently wait until the Redis daemon is ready for us.

Also, note that we manage monit from this place. We use monit for health and failover, so it is important that monit state is up-to-date and reflects the current state of Redis.

There is one more thing. With large data sets Redis wants to commit to a large chunk of memory. Sometimes this is actually too large to fit, and you will get complaints from a kernel (in our case Linux). To mitigate this in Linux you can do something like this:

```
echo 1 > /proc/sys/vm/overcommit_memory
```

SimpleDB

Managing the state of the Redis chain (cluster) we have to keep track of the following:

head
> Entry point for almost everything

nodes
> With master and slave, so we can follow the chain easily

tail
> New nodes can just use `slaveof(tail)`

If your client supports reading from slaves:

```
# Copyright (C) 2011, 2012 9apps B.V.
#
# This file is part of Redis for AWS.
#
# Redis for AWS is free software: you can redistribute it and/or modify
# it under the terms of the GNU General Public License as published by
# the Free Software Foundation, either version 3 of the License, or
# (at your option) any later version.
#
# Redis for AWS is distributed in the hope that it will be useful,
# but WITHOUT ANY WARRANTY; without even the implied warranty of
# MERCHANTABILITY or FITNESS FOR A PARTICULAR PURPOSE.  See the
```

```python
# GNU General Public License for more details.
#
# You should have received a copy of the GNU General Public License
# along with Redis for AWS. If not, see <http://www.gnu.org/licenses/>.


import os, sys, json, hashlib

from urllib2 import urlopen
from time import gmtime,strftime

from boto.sdb.connection import SDBConnection
from boto.sdb.regioninfo import RegionInfo


class Cluster:
    def __init__(self, key, access, cluster):
        userdata = json.loads(boto.utils.get_instance_userdata())
        metadata = boto.utils.get_instance_metadata()

        public_hostname = userdata['hostname']
        zone = userdata['availability-zone']
        region = zone[:-1]

        #us-east-1 breaks the convention. See http://docs.amazonwebservices.com/
general/latest/gr/rande.html#sdb_region
        endpoint = "sdb.{0}.amazonaws.com".format(region) if region != "us-
east-1" \
                else "sdb.amazonaws.com"
        region_info = RegionInfo(name=region, endpoint=endpoint)

        sdb = SDBConnection(key, access, region=region_info)

        self.domain = sdb.create_domain(cluster)

        self.metadata = self.domain.get_item('metadata', consistent_read=True)
        if None == self.metadata:
            self.metadata = self.domain.new_item('metadata')

            self.metadata.add_value('master', '')
            self.metadata.add_value('slave', '')
            self.metadata.save()

    def name(self):
        return self.domain.name

    def add_node(self, node, endpoint):
        try:
            head = self.metadata['master']
        except:
            head = ""
```

```python
        try:
            tail = self.metadata['slave']
        except:
            tail = ""

        # create a new node, always added to the tail
        new = self.domain.new_item(node)
        new.add_value('endpoint', endpoint)

        try:
            if head == tail == "":
                # we are empty; a cluster of one
                self.metadata['master'] = self.metadata['slave'] = node
            else:
                # now, we extend, by adding a new tail
                self.metadata['slave'] = node

                self.domain.put_attributes(node, {'master': head})
                self.domain.put_attributes(tail, {'slave': node})

                new.add_value('master', tail)

            self.metadata.save()
            new.save()
            return True
        except:
            # head or tail (perhaps both) are None?
            pass

        return False

    def delete_node(self, node):
        head = self.metadata['master']
        tail = self.metadata['slave']

        item = self.domain.get_item(node, True)

        if None != item:
            # we have to be careful, node might be head or tail
            if node == head == tail:
                self.metadata['master'] = None
                self.metadata['slave'] = None
            elif node == tail:
                master = self.get_master(node)
                self.metadata['slave'] = master
                self.domain.delete_attributes(master, ['slave'])
            elif node == head:
                slave = self.get_slave(node)
                self.metadata['master'] = slave
                self.domain.delete_attributes(slave, ['master'])
            else:
                master = self.get_master(node)
```

```
            slave = self.get_slave(node)

            self.domain.put_attributes(master, {'slave': slave})
            self.domain.put_attributes(slave, {'master': master})

        item.delete()
        self.metadata.save()
        return True
    else:
        return False


# blaming can be done in case of loss of connection. if a slave
# looses connection, it can blame its master, and start searching for
# a new master (or become THE master).
def incarcerate_node(self, node):
    head = self.metadata['master']
    tail = self.metadata['slave']

    item = self.domain.get_item(node, True)

    if None != item:
        # we have to be careful, node might be head or tail
        if node == head == tail:
            self.metadata['master'] = None
            self.metadata['slave'] = None
        elif node == tail:
            master = self.get_master(node)
            self.metadata['slave'] = master
            self.domain.delete_attributes(master, ['slave'])
        elif node == head:
            slave = self.get_slave(node)
            self.metadata['master'] = slave
            self.domain.delete_attributes(slave, ['master'])
        else:
            master = self.get_master(node)
            slave = self.get_slave(node)

            self.domain.put_attributes(master, {'slave': slave})
            self.domain.put_attributes(slave, {'master': master})

        self.domain.delete_attributes(node, ['master'])
        self.domain.delete_attributes(node, ['slave'])
        self.metadata.save()

        return True
    else:
        return False

def exists(self, node):
    return (self.domain.get_item(node, True) != None)

def get_endpoint(self, node):
```

```python
        try:
            return self.domain.get_item(node, True)['endpoint']
        except:
            return None

    def get_master(self, node=None):
        if node == None or node == "":
            return self.metadata['master']

        try:
            return self.domain.get_item(node, True)['master']
        except:
            return None

    def get_slave(self, node=None):
        if node == None or node == "":
            return self.metadata['slave']

        try:
            return self.domain.get_item(node, True)['slave']
        except:
            return None

    def size(self):
        select = "select count(*) from `{0}` where itemName() like '%.{0}'".for-
mat(self.domain.name)
        return int(self.domain.select(select, consistent_read=True).next()
['Count'])

    def check_integrity(self, cluster):
        pass

if __name__ == '__main__':
    key = os.environ['EC2_KEY_ID']
    access = os.environ['EC2_SECRET_KEY']

    # easy testing, use like this (requires environment variables)
    #        python cluster.py get_master cluster 2c922342a.cluster
    cluster = Cluster(key, access, sys.argv[2])
    print getattr(cluster, sys.argv[1])(*sys.argv[3:])
```

Redis cluster

Our cluster has one topology at the moment. We'll implement the cluster as a chain. The advantage of this is that the nodes are relatively independent. If a node is lost, it will be picked up by the slave, which moves itself up a place in the chain. Another advantage is that the slaves might lag, but the lag is always relative. Moving up is no problem; adding slaves is done at the tail.

The cluster's structure is managed in SimpleDB and made accessible using Route 53. The head of the chain is the *mydomain.com* and the tail is accessible through *tail.my domain.com*. Every individual node has a unique FQDN like *4821541d.mydomain.com*.

If your client supports reading from slaves, you can add support for getting them here. We didn't, as our apps do not need or support this (yet).

Route 53

Route 53 basically follows SimpleDB:

head
> Takes the name of the Redis cluster

nodes
> Every node has its unique, identifiable hostname

We don't need to get to tail from our apps, so we can skip keeping track of that in Route 53.

```
# Copyright (C) 2011, 2012 9apps B.V.
#
# This file is part of Redis for AWS.
#
# Redis for AWS is free software: you can redistribute it and/or modify
# it under the terms of the GNU General Public License as published by
# the Free Software Foundation, either version 3 of the License, or
# (at your option) any later version.
#
# Redis for AWS is distributed in the hope that it will be useful,
# but WITHOUT ANY WARRANTY; without even the implied warranty of
# MERCHANTABILITY or FITNESS FOR A PARTICULAR PURPOSE.  See the
# GNU General Public License for more details.
#
# You should have received a copy of the GNU General Public License
# along with Redis for AWS. If not, see <http://www.gnu.org/licenses/>.

import os, sys, platform
import json

from boto.route53.connection import Route53Connection
from boto.route53.record import ResourceRecordSets

class Route53Zone:
    def __init__(self, key, access, zone_id):
        self.zone_id = zone_id
        self.route53 = Route53Connection(key, access)

    def create_record(self, name, value):
        changes = ResourceRecordSets(self.route53, self.zone_id)

        change = changes.add_change("CREATE", name + ".", "CNAME", 60)
```

```
        change.add_value(value)
        changes.commit()

    def update_record(self, name, value):
        changes = ResourceRecordSets(self.route53, self.zone_id)

        sets = self.route53.get_all_rrsets(self.zone_id, None)
        for rset in sets:
            if rset.name == name + ".":
                previous_value = rset.resource_records[0]

                change = changes.add_change("DELETE", name + ".", "CNAME", 60)
                change.add_value(previous_value)

        change = changes.add_change("CREATE", name + ".", "CNAME", 60)
        change.add_value(value)
        changes.commit()

    def delete_record(self, name):
        changes = ResourceRecordSets(self.route53, self.zone_id)

        value = None
        sets = self.route53.get_all_rrsets(self.zone_id, None)
        for rset in sets:
            if rset.name == name + ".":
                value = rset.resource_records[0]

        if value != None:
            change = changes.add_change("DELETE", name + ".", "CNAME", 60)
            change.add_value(value)
            changes.commit()

if __name__ == '__main__':
    # easy testing, use like this (requires environment variables)
    #        python route53.py create_record key access id name value
    r53_zone = Route53Zone(sys.argv[2], sys.argv[3], sys.argv[4])
    print getattr(r53_zone, sys.argv[1])(*sys.argv[5:])
```

Failover

Failover in our cluster setup is managed by the slave. We know that every master has zero or one slave. And that a slave always has a master.

So, as a slave we monitor the master. If the master goes down we'll remove it, and we make ourselves slave of our *grandmaster*. Or, we assume head position and slaveof(no one).

```
# add this to the main monit with 'include <path>/redis.monitrc'

# always check the local redis
check process redis with pidfile /var/run/redis/redis.pid
  start program = "/etc/init.d/redis start"
```

```
stop program  = "/etc/init.d/redis stop"
if failed port 6379 for 3 times within 5 cycles then restart
group redis

set expectbuffer 2 kb
check host slave with address localhost
  if failed host localhost port 6379
    send "PING\r\nINFO\r\n" expect "role:slave"
    send "PING\r\nINFO\r\n" expect "master_link_status:up"
    3 cycles
  then exec "/root/ReDiS/remaster.sh"

check file initializing with path /var/run/redis/slave
  if does not exist then exec "/root/ReDiS/reslave.sh"
  else if succeeded then unmonitor
```

If a slave has to restore from a master with a sizable dataset it might take a while. Until it has caught up it is not fit to assume a master role, as it does not represent a valid slave. We use reslave.py for this:

```
# Copyright (C) 2011, 2012 9apps B.V.
#
# This file is part of Redis for AWS.
#
# Redis for AWS is free software: you can redistribute it and/or modify
# it under the terms of the GNU General Public License as published by
# the Free Software Foundation, either version 3 of the License, or
# (at your option) any later version.
#
# Redis for AWS is distributed in the hope that it will be useful,
# but WITHOUT ANY WARRANTY; without even the implied warranty of
# MERCHANTABILITY or FITNESS FOR A PARTICULAR PURPOSE.  See the
# GNU General Public License for more details.
#
# You should have received a copy of the GNU General Public License
# along with Redis for AWS. If not, see <http://www.gnu.org/licenses/>.

import os, sys, redis

from cluster import Cluster
from host import Host
from route53 import Route53Zone

from events import Events

# your amazon keys
key = os.environ['EC2_KEY_ID']
access = os.environ['EC2_SECRET_KEY']

# what is the domain to work with
name = os.environ['REDIS_NAME'].strip()
zone_name = os.environ['HOSTED_ZONE_NAME'].rstrip('.')
```

```
zone_id = os.environ['HOSTED_ZONE_ID']

# the name (and identity) of the cluster (the master)
cluster = "{0}.{1}".format(name, zone_name)

# get/create the cluster environment
cluster = Cluster(key, access, cluster)

events = Events(key, access, cluster.name())
host = Host(cluster.name(), events)
node = host.get_node()
endpoint = host.get_endpoint()
component = os.path.basename(sys.argv[0])
def log(message, logging='info'):
    events.log(node, component, message, logging)

r = redis.StrictRedis(host='localhost', port=6379)

if __name__ == '__main__':
    try:
        log('get Redis INFO', 'info')
        info = r.info()

        log('get the link_status', 'info')
        if 'master_link_status' in info:
            log('determine if our master is up', 'info')
            if info['master_link_status'] == "up":
                log('master is up: touch the slave', 'info')
                os.system('/bin/touch /var/run/redis/slave')

    except Exception as e:
        log('no redis yet?', 'info')
```

The main part of failover is done in `remaster.py`:

```
# Copyright (C) 2011, 2012 9apps B.V.
#
# This file is part of Redis for AWS.
#
# Redis for AWS is free software: you can redistribute it and/or modify
# it under the terms of the GNU General Public License as published by
# the Free Software Foundation, either version 3 of the License, or
# (at your option) any later version.
#
# Redis for AWS is distributed in the hope that it will be useful,
# but WITHOUT ANY WARRANTY; without even the implied warranty of
# MERCHANTABILITY or FITNESS FOR A PARTICULAR PURPOSE.  See the
# GNU General Public License for more details.
#
# You should have received a copy of the GNU General Public License
# along with Redis for AWS. If not, see <http://www.gnu.org/licenses/>.

import os, sys, redis
```

```python
from cluster import Cluster
from host import Host
from route53 import Route53Zone

from events import Events

# your amazon keys
key = os.environ['EC2_KEY_ID']
access = os.environ['EC2_SECRET_KEY']

# what is the domain to work with
name = os.environ['REDIS_NAME'].strip()
zone_name = os.environ['HOSTED_ZONE_NAME'].rstrip('.')
zone_id = os.environ['HOSTED_ZONE_ID']

# the name (and identity) of the cluster (the master)
cluster = "{0}.{1}".format(name, zone_name)

# get/create the cluster environment
cluster = Cluster(key, access, cluster)
r53_zone = Route53Zone(key, access, zone_id)

events = Events(key, access, cluster.name())
host = Host(cluster.name(), events)
node = host.get_node()
endpoint = host.get_endpoint()
component = os.path.basename(sys.argv[0])
def log(message, logging='info'):
    events.log(node, component, message, logging)

r = redis.StrictRedis(host='localhost', port=6379)

if __name__ == '__main__':
    # make sure we get the redis master, perhaps our master is already gone
    # from the cluster
    try:
        log('get Redis INFO', 'info')
        info = r.info()
        log('get the link_status', 'info')
        link_status = info['master_link_status']

        log('determine if our master is up', 'info')
        if link_status != "up":
            log('how long are we down?', 'info')
            link_down_since_seconds = info['master_link_down_since_seconds']
            master_sync_in_progress = info['master_sync_in_progress']

            # if not syncing, and link down longer than 30s
            down = ((master_sync_in_progress == 0) and
                            (link_down_since_seconds > 30))
        else:
```

```
                down = False

        except Exception as e:
            log('master are down, or we were master, in any case we should not be
    here ', 'info')
            down = True


        if down:
            log('down: find a new master!', 'info')
            try:
                master = r.info()['master_host']
                log("master: {0}".format(master), 'info')
                if cluster.exists(master):
                    grandmaster = cluster.get_master(master)
                        log("{0} = cluster.get_master({1})".format(grandmaster, mas-
    ter), 'info')

                    # and make sure the master doesn't participate anymore
                    cluster.incarcerate_node(master)
                    log("cluster.incarcerate_node({0})".format(master), 'info')
                else:
                    grandmaster = cluster.get_master(node)
                      log("{0} = cluster.get_master({1})".format(grandmaster, node),
    'info')
            except:
                log('we never were a slave', 'info')
                grandmaster = None

            if grandmaster == None:
                r53_zone.update_record(cluster.name(), endpoint)
                    log("r53_zone.update_record({0}, {1})".format(cluster.name(), end-
    point), 'info')
                host.set_master()
                log("host.set_master()", 'info')
            else:
                host.set_master(grandmaster)
                log("host.set_master({0})".format(grandmaster), 'info')
        else:
            log("master is up (and running)", 'info')
```

In Practice

Redis is interesting, but in practice you have to be very gentle with it. Large datasets are
difficult to handle, as slaving takes quite some time (because there is no incremental
slaveof).

Also, as we mentioned before, we have dropped persistence altogether in high traffic environments. We rely instead on replication and failover.

With this setup we can easily scale up. We rotate a Redis cluster one by one, relying on the failover mechanism we have just built. This is also a good test of whether the application handles these failovers gracefully or whether it comes grindingly to a halt.

## CHAPTER 9

Logstash

Managing logs is difficult. It gets even more complicated when your infrastructure is bigger. And, making it dynamic (changing instances, all the time) doesn't help at all.

You have commercial services like Splunk and Loggly, but they can get very expensive, very quickly. We would prefer to run it ourselves, providing that the following are true:

- We can design this to be reliable.
- It has a small footprint for log shipping.
- It comes with out of the box interface for reading (analyzing).
- It is scalable.

Logstash (*http://logstash.net/*) calls itself a log management solution. You can collect events, parse them (add meaning), search, and store them. Logstash can be easily de-coupled, and run in a setup (see Figure 9-1).

The base setup should be able to handle several hundred events per second. The shippers have a small footprint. The reader (and interface) run on high CPU medium. For the elasticsearch (powering the interface) we'll use two high memory medium instances.

Build

Logstash works with `input`, `filter`, and `output` definitions. Most of the time shippers read from file (`input`), do not filter very much, and write out to a middleware message bus (`output`). Logstash comes with many plug-ins.

The default isolated message bus is RabbitMQ; you can also use Redis, but we want to use SQS, of course.

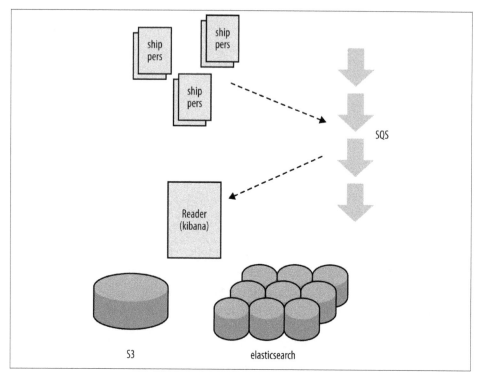

Figure 9-1. Logstash distributed logging

The latest logstash.jar comes with the AWS SDK. This means we do not have to build a custom jar anymore.

Shipper

The shipper reads from file and writes to SQS. A typical shipper configuration looks like this:

```
input {
  file {
    type => "linux-syslog"

    # Wildcards work, here :)
    path => [ "/var/log/*.log", "/var/log/messages", "/var/log/syslog" ]
  }

  file {
    type => "nginx-access"
    path => "/var/log/nginx/access.log"
  }
```

```
  file {
    type => "nginx-error"
    path => "/var/log/nginx/error.log"
  }

  file {
    type => "fashiolista"
    path => "/var/log/fashiolista/*.log"
  }
}

output {
  # Emit events to stdout for easy debugging of what is going through
  # logstash.
  stdout { }

  sqs {
    access_key_id => ""
    secret_access_key => ""
    name => ""
    endpoint => "sqs.us-east-1.amazonaws.com"
  }
}
```

Output Plug-in

```
require "logstash/outputs/base"
require "logstash/namespace"

require 'aws-sdk'

class LogStash::Outputs::SQS < LogStash::Outputs::Base
  config_name "sqs"
  plugin_status "beta"

  config :access_key_id, :validate => :string, :required => true
  config :secret_access_key, :validate => :string, :required => true
  config :name, :validate => :string, :required => true
  config :endpoint, :validate => :string, :required => true,
         :default => 'sqs.eu-west-1.amazonaws.com'

  public
  def register
    # if you work with IAM, allow sqs:* on only this queue
    # aws-sdk appears to be pretty particular in their understanding
    # of IAM in combination with SQS (see iam.sqs.policy)
    @queue = create()
  end # def register

  public
  def receive(event)
    return unless output?(event)
```

```
      @queue.send_message(event.to_json)
    rescue
      # create (if not exists), but wait for 60s first
      sleep(60)
      @queue.send_message(event.to_json)
    end # def receive

    private
    def create()
      sqs = AWS::SQS.new(
            :access_key_id => @access_key_id,
            :secret_access_key => @secret_access_key,
            :sqs_endpoint => @endpoint)

      sqs.queues.create(@name)
    end
  end # class LogStash::Outputs::SQS
```

Reader

The reader does most of the heavy lifting. It needs to keep the queues empty, parse them, and add them to elasticsearch. You want to keep your logs forever, and you even want the reader to store your logs on disk.

Spot instances

The reader is relatively fault tolerant. We expose it using ELB, and data is persisted in SQS and elasticsearch. We could run this as a Spot Instance. Perhaps we could even choose our bid price to reflect office hours, as logstash might not be required outside of office hours.

This is a typical reader configuration:

```
input {
  sqs {
    type => "sqs"
    access_key_id => ""
    secret_access_key => ""
    name => "logstash-django-rawlogs"
    endpoint => "sqs.eu-west-1.amazonaws.com"
  }
}

filter {
  grok {
    type => "nginx"
    tags => [ "access" ]
```

```
    patterns_dir => "/usr/local/logstash/patterns"
      pattern => "%{HOST:servername} %{IP:clientip} (?:%{HOST:clienthost}|-) (?:%
{USER:clientuser}|-) \[%{HTTPDATE:time}\] \"(?:%{WORD:verb} %{URIPATHPARAM:re-
quest} HTTP/%{NUMBER:httpversion}|%{DATA:unparsedrq})\" %{NUMBER:response} (?:%
{NUMBER:bytes}|-)              (?:%{QUOTEDSTRING:httpreferrer}|-)              (?:%
{QUOTEDSTRING:httpuseragent}|-)    (?:%{NUMBER:cookieid}|-)    \"%{NUMBER:reques-
ttime} (?:%{NUMBER:upstreamresponsetime}( : %{NUMBER})*|-)\""
  }

  mutate {
    convert => [ "requesttime", "float" ]
  }

  # collapse the stack traces
  multiline {
    type => "django"
    pattern => "^( |Traceback|AssertionError)"
    what => "previous"
  }
}

output {
  #stdout { }
  elasticsearch {
    cluster => "logstash.elasticsearch"
    host => "logstash.elasticsearch.goteam.be"
    port => 9300
    index => "logstash-%{+YYYY.MM.dd}"
  }
}
```

Input Plug-in

```
require 'json'

require "logstash/inputs/base"
require "logstash/namespace"

require 'aws-sdk'

java_import java.util.concurrent.Executors

class LogStash::Inputs::SQS < LogStash::Inputs::Base
  config_name "sqs"
  plugin_status "beta"

  config :access_key_id, :validate => :string, :required => true
  config :secret_access_key, :validate => :string, :required => true
  config :name, :validate => :string, :required => true
  config :endpoint, :validate => :string, :required => true,
         :default => 'sqs.eu-west-1.amazonaws.com'
  config :threads, :validate => :number, :default => 32
```

```
def initialize(*args)
  super(*args)
  @format ||= "json_event"
end # def initialize

public
def register
  # if you work with IAM, allow sqs:* on only this queue
  # aws-sdk appears to be pretty particular in their understanding
  # of IAM in combination with SQS (see iam.sqs.policy)
  @queue = create()

  @pool = Executors.newFixedThreadPool(@threads)
end # def register

public
def run(queue)
  @threads.times do
    @pool.submit do
      @queue.poll(:batch_size => 10) do |msg|
        queue << to_event( msg.body, msg.queue)
      end
    end
  end
end # def run

private
def create()
  sqs = AWS::SQS.new(
          :access_key_id => @access_key_id,
          :secret_access_key => @secret_access_key,
          :sqs_endpoint => @endpoint)

  sqs.queues.create(@name)
end
end # class LogStash::Inputs::SQS
```

Grok

This is one of the more powerful features of logstash. It uses Google Grok to parse an event (a group of log lines) into fields. These fields are stored separately and make it very easy to search or do other more complex operations.

It might take a while to get the hang of this, and it is quite tedious to build the more complex Grok filters. But the results are very valuable.

Kibana

As an interface we use kibana (*https://github.com/rashidkpc/Kibana*). The main kibana page looks like this:

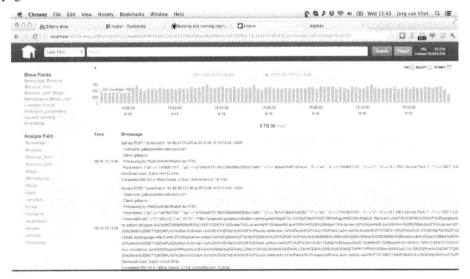

You can quickly get particular distribution scores on the fields you have, standard or added with your grok patterns.

Kibana exposes elasticsearch's very powerful search features. You can create your queries by hand or you can select the fields from the events.

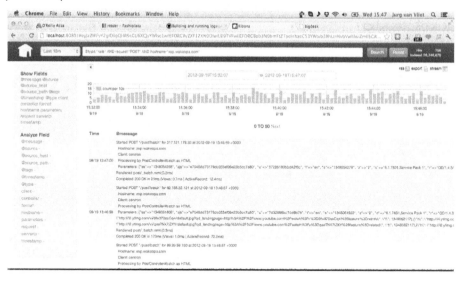

## CHAPTER 10

Global (Content) Delivery

A global operation is a blessing in disguise. Some things are not easy to solve. But if you do, you have the opportunity to achieve the next level of Resilience and Reliability.

AWS offers two services you can use for global delivery. It has CloudFront, their Content Distribution Network, and it has Route 53, a global DNS network.

CloudFront

A full treatise of CloudFront is beyond the scope of this book. We use it in several different ways.

We use CloudFront to expose objects in S3 buckets. This is easy, and it automatically distributes the objects to multiple locations all around the world.

You can also use CloudFront on a *Custom Origin*. This basically means that you point the CloudFront distribution to a site (which can be an S3 bucket), and then you can set a *default object*, for example `index.html`, and you are good to go.

With the introduction of more caching flexibility it is quite feasible to have your dynamic content pass through CloudFront as well. We do not do this very often yet.

(Live) Streaming

CloudFront has another remarkable feature, and that is streaming. The feature itself is not that sophisticated, but it is offered at the same price as normal content delivery.

For live streaming there are several examples. But for the Concertgebouw (the concert hall in Amsterdam) we had to do something else. One of the requirements was to stream at multiple bit rates, dynamically chosen by client. And one other requirement was that we had to deal with *interlaced* material coming in.

We will spare you the details, but the usual Flash Media Server setup was not sufficient. The transcoding (transformation of one high quality stream into multiple streams of different qualities) had to be moved to AWS as well.

So, we ended up adapting the Flash Media Server (FMS) streaming example. We added a Wowza server for transcoding, feeding the streams automatically into FMS, which was picked up by CloudFront.

Asynchronous transcoding

Our challenge is to transcode live. If you are tasked with transcoding asynchronously you can use a different setup. You can use SQS (or SWF) to produce/consume transcoding tasks. The consumers (the transcoders) can easily run on Spot Instances to reduce the cost.

Wowza

Wowza is like FMS—it doesn't play nicely with CloudFront yet, but it does do a good job of encoding. However, we had to make the whole setup very flexible. For two events a month (to start with) it doesn't make sense to have two very expensive machines running around the clock.

The first thing we had to fix was automatically pushing the published streams to a particular location. Wowza has a plug-in framework we used for that.

```
package com.videodock.wms.modules;

import java.io.BufferedReader;
import java.io.File;
import java.io.FileInputStream;
import java.io.InputStream;
import java.io.InputStreamReader;
import java.net.MalformedURLException;
import java.net.URL;
import java.util.HashMap;
import java.util.Map;

import com.google.gson.Gson;
import com.wowza.wms.amf.AMFPacket;
import com.wowza.wms.application.IApplicationInstance;
import com.wowza.wms.logging.WMSLoggerFactory;
import com.wowza.wms.module.ModuleBase;
import com.wowza.wms.plugin.pushpublish.protocol.rtmp.PushPublisherRTMP;
import com.wowza.wms.stream.IMediaStream;
import com.wowza.wms.stream.IMediaStreamActionNotify2;

public class PushPublisher extends ModuleBase {
    Map<IMediaStream, PushPublisherRTMP> publishers = new HashMap<IMediaStream,
PushPublisherRTMP>();
```

```java
class UserData {
    private String key;
    private String event;

    UserData() {
        // no-args constructor
    }

    public String getKey() {
        return key;
    }

    public void setKey(String key) {
        this.key = key;
    }

    public String getEvent() {
        return event;
    }

    public void setEvent(String event) {
        this.event = event;
    }
}

class StreamNotify implements IMediaStreamActionNotify2 {

    public void onPlay(IMediaStream stream, String streamName,
            double playStart, double playLen, int playReset) {
    }

    public void onPause(IMediaStream stream, boolean isPause,
            double location) {
    }

    public void onSeek(IMediaStream stream, double location) {
    }

    public void onStop(IMediaStream stream) {
    }

    public void onMetaData(IMediaStream stream, AMFPacket metaDataPacket) {
    }

    public void onPauseRaw(IMediaStream stream, boolean isPause,
            double location) {
    }

    public void onPublish(IMediaStream stream, String streamName,
            boolean isRecord, boolean isAppend) {
        if (stream.isTranscodeResult()) {
```

```
        try {
            IApplicationInstance appInstance = stream.getStreams()
                    .getAppInstance();

            synchronized (publishers) {
                PushPublisherRTMP publisher = new PushPublisherRTMP();

                // Source stream
                publisher.setAppInstance(appInstance);
                publisher.setSrcStreamName(streamName);

                // Destination stream
                publisher.setHostname(getEvent() + ".cgb.videodock.eu");
                publisher.setPort(1935);
                publisher.setDstApplicationName(appInstance
                        .getApplication().getName());

                // setConnectionQueryString() does not appear to work.
                // appending it to the streamName like this gets
                // everything through to the other side (FMS)
                publisher.setConnectionQueryStr(stream.getQueryStr());

                String queryStr;
                if (stream.isTranscodeResult()) {
                    String streamSrcName = stream.getName().substring(
                            0, stream.getName().indexOf("_"));
                    getLogger().error("Source Stream Name: " + stream-
SrcName);

                    IMediaStream streamSrc = stream.getStreams()
                            .getStream(streamSrcName);
                    if (!"".equals(streamSrc.getQueryStr())) {
                        queryStr = streamName
                                + "?"
                                + streamSrc.getQueryStr().substring(
                                        streamSrc.getQueryStr()
                                                .indexOf("?") + 1,
                                        streamSrc.getQueryStr()
                                                .length());
                    } else {
                        queryStr = streamName;
                    }
                    getLogger().error(
                            "Source Stream Query String: " + queryStr);
                } else {
                    if (!"".equals(stream.getQueryStr())) {
                        queryStr = streamName + "?"
                                + stream.getQueryStr();
                    } else {
                        queryStr = streamName;
                    }
                }
```

```java
                    getLogger().error("queryString: " + queryStr);
                    stream.getProperties().setProperty("queryString",
                            queryStr);
                    publisher.setDstStreamName(queryStr);
                    stream.setQueryStr(queryStr);

                    publisher
                            .setConnectionFlashVerion(PushPublisherRTMP.CUR-
RENTFMLEVERSION);

                    publisher.setSendFCPublish(true);
                    publisher.setSendReleaseStream(true);
                    publisher.setSendOnMetadata(true);
                    publisher.setDebugLog(true);
                    publisher.setDebugPackets(false);

                    publisher.connect();
                    publishers.put(stream, publisher);
                }
            } catch (Exception e) {
                WMSLoggerFactory.getLogger(null).error(
                        "ModulePushPublishSimpleExample#StreamNotify.onPub-
lish: "
                            + e.toString());
            }
        }
    }

    public void onUnPublish(IMediaStream stream, String streamName,
            boolean isRecord, boolean isAppend) {
        stopPublisher(stream);
    }
}

    public void stopPublisher(IMediaStream stream) {
        try {
            synchronized (publishers) {
                PushPublisherRTMP publisher = publishers.remove(stream);
                if (publisher != null) {
                    publisher.disconnect();
                }
            }
        } catch (Exception e) {
            WMSLoggerFactory.getLogger(null).error(
                    "ModulePushPublishSimpleExample#StreamNotify.onPublish: "
                        + e.toString());
        }
    }

    public void onStreamCreate(IMediaStream stream) {
        stream.addClientListener(new StreamNotify());
```

```
        }

        public void onStreamDestroy(IMediaStream stream) {
            stopPublisher(stream);
        }

        private String getEvent() {
            String event = "webcast";
            Gson gson = new Gson();

            try {
                // URL url = new URL("http://169.254.169.254/latest/user-data/");
                FileInputStream file = new FileInputStream(new File(
                        "/etc/default/wowza.json"));

                // InputStream response = url.openStream();
                BufferedReader reader = new BufferedReader(new InputStreamReader(
                        file));

                event = gson.fromJson(reader, UserData.class).getEvent();

                reader.close();
            } catch (MalformedURLException e) {
                // TODO Auto-generated catch block
                e.printStackTrace();
            }

            return event;
        }
    }
```

CloudFormation

Because we will do one or two events per month at first, we want to have a very temporary infrastructure. We will probably use it about 8 hours per event. The assets we run are pretty big, m2.4xlarge and c1.xlarge. These machines costs several hundreds of dollars per month.

We don't see the benefit of CloudFormation often in our projects, but this is a good example of where it is perfect. The CloudFormation template is an adapted version of Adobe's template for streaming with (FMS) and CloudFront.

In this template you can see several interesting things we can automate. You see the use of Route53, for accessibility. You see the extensive use of userdata scripting, mainly because we have to massage FMS into shape every time we launch. (We can't make an AMI from their instance.)

The resulting template will take a number of parameters. It will launch a Wowza instance (we do m2.4xlarge). This instance will register itself with the supplied license key, get some configuration files determining the transcoding scheme.

Then it will launch the FMS, where we have to do several additional things as well. We are not so happy with the default `main.far` which handles publishing and several other things. So we remove that and add our own `main.asc`. And we create and provision an *event* with configuration files from an S3 bucket.

```
{
  "AWSTemplateFormatVersion" : "2010-09-09",

  "Description" : "Create a Videodock Live Streaming Stack (Wowza & FMS)",

  "Parameters" : {
    "KeyName" : {
      "Description" : "Name of and existing EC2 KeyPair to enable SSH access to
the instances",
      "Default" : "cgb",
      "Type" : "String"
    },
    "LicenseKey" : {
      "Description" : "License key for Wowza media server",
      "Type" : "String",
      "Default" : "SVRD3-zn6Xb-bupeY-7TNmT-ZXhMm-4xABM",
      "NoEcho" : "true"
    },
    "EventName" : {
      "Description" : "Name the default event",
      "Type" : "String",
      "Default" : "webcast"
    },
    "StreamName" : {
        "Type" : "String",
        "Description" : "A short name for your live stream (no spaces allowed).
Default value is livestream.",
        "Default"     : "livestream"
    },
    "WowzaInstanceType" : {
        "Type"                   : "String",
        "Description"            : "The type of Amazon EC2 instance to launch.
Valid values are: m1.small, m1.medium, c1.medium, m1.large, m1.xlarge,
m2.xlarge, m2.2xlarge, m2.4xlarge, c1.xlarge, hi1.4xlarge.",
        "Default"                : "m1.large",
          "AllowedValues"              : [ "m1.small","m1.medium","c1.medi-
um","m1.large","m1.xlarge","m2.xlarge","m2.2xlarge","m2.4xlarge","c1.xlarge","hi
1.4xlarge" ],
        "ConstraintDescription" : "must be a valid Amazon EC2 instance type."
    },
    "FMSAdminUsername" : {
        "Type" : "String",
        "Description" : "Enter a username you want to use for the Flash Media
Administration Console. Default value is admin.",
        "Default"     : "admin"
    },
    "FMSAdminPassword" : {
```

```
        "Type"                    : "String",
        "NoEcho"                  : "true",
        "MinLength"               : "8",
        "MaxLength"               : "40",
        "AllowedPattern"          : "[a-zA-Z0-9]*",
        "Default"                 : "12345678",
         "Description"                    : "Enter an alphanumeric password (minimum 8
characters) you want to use for the Flash Media Administration Console.",
        "ConstraintDescription" : "must contain only alphanumeric characters
and minimum 8 characters."
    },
    "FMSInstanceType" : {
        "Type"                    : "String",
        "Description"                : "The type of Amazon EC2 instance to launch.
Valid values are: m1.large, m1.xlarge, m2.xlarge, m2.2xlarge, m2.4xlarge,
c1.xlarge.",
        "Default"                    : "m1.large",
                "AllowedValues"                               :
[ "m1.large","m1.xlarge","m2.xlarge","m2.2xlarge","m2.4xlarge","c1.xlarge" ],
        "ConstraintDescription" : "must be a valid Amazon EC2 instance type."
    }
  },

  "Mappings" : {
    "WowzaRegionMap" : {
      "eu-west-1" : {
        "AMI" : "ami-2f57565b"
      }
    },
    "FMSRegionMap" : {
        "us-east-1"       : { "AMI" : "ami-69f82600" },
        "us-west-2"       : { "AMI" : "ami-c8de52f8" },
        "us-west-1"       : { "AMI" : "ami-a3b7efe6" },
        "eu-west-1"       : { "AMI" : "ami-dd073fa9" },
        "ap-southeast-1" : { "AMI" : "ami-904f08c2" },
        "ap-northeast-1" : { "AMI" : "ami-b06edfb1" },
        "sa-east-1"       : { "AMI" : "ami-bebf61a3" }
    }
  },

  "Resources" : {
    "WowzaInstance" : {
      "Type" : "AWS::EC2::Instance",
      "Properties" : {
        "SecurityGroups" : [ { "Ref" : "WowzaSecurityGroup" } ],
        "KeyName" : { "Ref" : "KeyName" },
        "ImageId" : { "Fn::FindInMap" : [ "WowzaRegionMap", { "Ref" : "AWS::Re-
gion" }, "AMI" ]},
        "Monitoring" : "true",
        "InstanceType" : {"Ref" : "WowzaInstanceType"},
        "Tags" : [ {
          "Key" : "Name",
```

```
                "Value" : { "Fn::Join" : [ "", [ "wowza.", { "Ref" : "EventName" },
".cgb.videodock.eu" ]]}
          } ],
          "UserData" : { "Fn::Base64" : { "Fn::Join" : [ "", [
                    "#!/bin/bash",
              "\n", "/bin/echo \"", { "Ref" : "LicenseKey" } , "\" > /usr/local/
WowzaMediaServer/conf/Server.license",
              "\n",
              "\n", "/usr/bin/curl --silent \\",
                "\n", "    https://s3-eu-west-1.amazonaws.com/cgb.videodock.eu/
wowza/", { "Ref" : "EventName" }, "/transcoder/templates/transrate.xml > \\",
                "\n", "    /usr/local/WowzaMediaServer/transcoder/templates/trans-
rate.xml",
              "\n", "/usr/bin/curl --silent \\",
                "\n", "    https://s3-eu-west-1.amazonaws.com/cgb.videodock.eu/
wowza/", { "Ref" : "EventName" }, "/conf/livepkgr/Application.xml > \\",
                "\n", "    /usr/local/WowzaMediaServer/conf/livepkgr/Applica-
tion.xml",
              "\n", "/bin/cat > /etc/default/wowza.json <<EOFF",
              "\n", "{",
              "\n", " \"event\" : \"", { "Ref" : "EventName" }, "\",",
              "\n", " \"key\" : \"", { "Ref" : "LicenseKey" } , "\"",
              "\n", "}",
              "\n", "EOFF",
              "\n", "sleep 15 && /etc/init.d/WowzaMediaServer start"
          ] ] } }
        }
      },

    "WowzaSecurityGroup" : {
      "Type" : "AWS::EC2::SecurityGroup",
      "Properties" : {
        "GroupDescription" : "Security group for the Wowza media server",
        "SecurityGroupIngress" : [
              {"IpProtocol" : "tcp", "FromPort" : "22", "ToPort" : "22", "Ci-
drIp" : "0.0.0.0/0"},
              {"IpProtocol" : "tcp", "FromPort" : "80", "ToPort" : "80", "Ci-
drIp" : "0.0.0.0/0"},
              {"IpProtocol" : "tcp", "FromPort" : "1111", "ToPort" : "1111", "Ci-
drIp" : "0.0.0.0/0"},
              {"IpProtocol" : "tcp", "FromPort" : "1935", "ToPort" : "1935", "Ci-
drIp" : "0.0.0.0/0"},
              {"IpProtocol" : "udp", "FromPort" : "1935", "ToPort" : "1935", "Ci-
drIp" : "0.0.0.0/0"}
          ]
        }
      },
      "WowzaDNSRecord" : {
        "Type" : "AWS::Route53::RecordSet",
        "Properties" : {
          "HostedZoneName" : "cgb.videodock.eu.",
          "Comment" : "Wowza streaming entry point.",
```

```
                "Name" : { "Fn::Join" : [ "", [ "wowza.", { "Ref" : "EventName" },
".cgb.videodock.eu" ]]},
            "Type" : "CNAME",
            "TTL" : "60",
                "ResourceRecords" : [
                    {"Fn::GetAtt":["WowzaInstance","PublicDnsName"]}
                ]
        }
    },

    "LiveStreamingDistribution" : {
        "Type" : "AWS::CloudFront::Distribution",
        "Properties" : {
            "DistributionConfig" : {
                "CustomOrigin" : {
                    "DNSName"                   : { "Fn::GetAtt" : [ "FMSOriginServ-
er", "PublicDnsName" ] },
                    "HTTPPort"              : "80",
                    "HTTPSPort"             : "443",
                    "OriginProtocolPolicy" : "http-only"
                },
                "Enabled" : "true",
                "Logging" : {
                    "Bucket" : "logs.cgb.videodock.eu.s3.amazonaws.com",
                    "Prefix" : { "Ref" : "EventName" }
                },
                    "CNAMEs" : [ { "Fn::Join" : [ "", [ "cdn.", { "Ref" : "Even-
tName" }, ".cgb.videodock.eu" ]]} ],
                "Comment" : "Live HTTP Streaming"
            }

        }
    },

    "FMSOriginServer" : {
        "Type" : "AWS::EC2::Instance",
        "Properties" : {
            "SecurityGroups" : [ { "Ref" : "FMSOriginServerSecurityGroup" } ],
            "KeyName"        : { "Ref" : "KeyName" },
            "ImageId"        : { "Fn::FindInMap" : [ "FMSRegionMap", { "Ref" :
"AWS::Region" }, "AMI" ]},
            "Monitoring" : "true",
            "InstanceType"   : {"Ref" : "FMSInstanceType"},
                "Tags" : [ {
                    "Key" : "Name",
                    "Value" : { "Fn::Join" : [ "", [ { "Ref" : "EventName" },
".cgb.videodock.eu" ]]}
                } ],
            "UserData" : { "Fn::Base64" : { "Fn::Join" : [ "", [
                    "#!/bin/bash",
                "\n", "sed -i \"s/^SERVER.ADMIN_USERNAME.*=/SERVER.ADMIN_USER-
NAME = ", { "Ref" : "FMSAdminUsername" },"/\" /opt/adobe/fms/conf/fms.ini",
```

```
                    "\n", "sed -i \"s/^SERVER.ADMINSERVER_HOSTPORT.*=/SERVER.ADMIN-
SERVER_HOSTPORT = :1111/\" /opt/adobe/fms/conf/fms.ini",
                    "\n", "chown fmsuser:fmsgroup /opt/adobe/fms/conf/fms.ini",
                    "\n", "/opt/adobe/fms/fmsmgr adminserver stop",
                    "\n", "echo \"", { "Ref" : "FMSAdminPassword" },"\" | /opt/
adobe/fms/fmsadmin -console -user ", { "Ref" : "FMSAdminUsername" },
                    "\n", "/opt/adobe/fms/fmsmgr adminserver start",
                    "\n", "cat > /mnt/webroot/crossdomain.xml <<EOFF",
                    "\n", "<?xml version=\"1.0\"?>",
                    "\n", " <cross-domain-policy>",
                    "\n", " <site-control permitted-cross-domain-policies=\"master-
only\" />",
                    "\n", " <allow-access-from domain=\"*.osmf.org\" />",
                    "\n", " <allow-access-from domain=\"*.adobe.com\" />",
                    "\n", " <allow-access-from domain=\"*.macromedia.com\" />",
                    "\n", " <allow-access-from domain=\"*.videodock.com\" />",
                    "\n", "</cross-domain-policy>",
                    "\n", "EOFF",
                    "\n", "chown fmsuser:fmsgroup /mnt/webroot/crossdomain.xml",
                    "\n", "rm /mnt/applications/livepkgr/main.far",
                    "\n", "cat <<EOF > /mnt/applications/livepkgr/main.asc",
                    "\n", "application.onAppStart = function()",
                    "\n", "{",
                    "\n", "    trace(\"Application name: \" + applica-
tion.name);",
                    "\n", "    trace(\"Server: \" + application.server);",
                    "\n", "    _clientId = 0;",
                    "\n", "    ",
                    "\n", "    application.s = new Array();",
                    "\n", "    application.a = new Array();",
                    "\n", "    application.v = new Array();",
                    "\n", "}",
                    "\n", "",
                    "\n", "application.onStatus = function()",
                    "\n", "{",
                    "\n", "    /*trace(\"There is an error in the code or
functionality.\");*/",
                    "\n", "}",
                    "\n", "",
                    "\n", "application.onConnect = function(clientObj)",
                    "\n", "{",
                    "\n", "    this.acceptConnection(clientObj);",
                    "\n", "}",
                    "\n", "",
                    "\n", "Stream.prototype.trace = function(msg)",
                    "\n", "{",
                    "\n", "    trace(this.type + \":\" + this.name + \" - \" +
msg);",
                    "\n", "}",
                    "\n", "",
                    "\n", "application.onPublish = function(clientObj, stream-
Obj)",
```

```
                    "\n", "{",
                        "\n", "        // a race can happen during republish. if
onPublish is called",
                        "\n", "        // before onUnpublish, we need to wait for
onUnpublish to",
                    "\n", "        // complete before calling onPublish for the new
stream.",
                    "\n", "        if (streamObj.publishing == true)",
                    "\n", "        {",
                    "\n", "            // onUnpublish has not been called yet",
                    "\n", "            //trace(\"Unpublish pending...\");",
                        "\n", "            streamObj.publishingClient = clientObj; //
save and call onPublish later",
                    "\n", "            return;",
                    "\n", "        }",
                    "\n", "        streamObj.publishing = true;",
                    "\n", "        trace(\"onPublish : \" + streamObj.name);",
                    "\n", "",
                    "\n", "        var queryString = streamObj.publishQueryString;",
                    "\n", "        var liveEventName = streamObj.name;",
                    "\n", "        var audioStreamSrc = \"\";",
                    "\n", "        var audioStreamName = \"\";",
                    "\n", "        var videoStreamSrc = \"\";",
                    "\n", "        var videoStreamName = \"\";",
                    "\n", "        var recordMode = \"append\";",
                    "\n", "",
                        "\n", "        //trace(\"queryString[\"+queryString+\"]
stream[\"+streamObj.name+\"]\");",
                        "\n", "        if (queryString == undefined || (queryString.lo-
caleCompare(\"\") == 0)) {",
                        "\n", "            /* Did not find query string so use the
streamname as the event id */",
                        "\n", "            trace(\"Query string not specified. Using
StreamName[\"",
                    "\n", "                +liveEventName+\"] as eventname\");",
                    "\n", "        } else {",
                        "\n", "            /* Looking for name value pair adbe-live-
event in the query string. If specified, use event name based on it. Otherwise,
it is a single stream so you don't need to configure Event.xml and Manifest.xml
*/",
                    "\n", "            var nvpairs = new LoadVars();",
                    "\n", "            nvpairs.decode(queryString);",
                    "\n", "            for (var nv in nvpairs) {",
                    "\n", "                var nval = nvpairs[nv];",
                        "\n", "                /*trace(\"nv[\"+nv+\"]=val[\"+nval+\"]
\");*/",
                        "\n", "                if (nv.localeCompare(\"adbe-live-event
\")==0) {",
                    "\n", "                    liveEventName = nval;",
                        "\n", "                    /*trace(\"live event set to[\"+liveE-
ventName+\"]\");*/",
                    "\n", "                }",
```

```
            "\n", "            else if (nv.localeCompare(\"adbe-audio-
stream-src\") == 0)",
            "\n", "            {",
            "\n", "                audioStreamSrc = nval;",
            "\n", "            }",
            "\n", "            else if (nv.localeCompare(\"adbe-audio-
stream-name\") == 0)",
            "\n", "            {",
            "\n", "                audioStreamName = nval;",
            "\n", "            }",
            "\n", "            else if (nv.localeCompare(\"adbe-video-
stream-src\") == 0)",
            "\n", "            {",
            "\n", "                videoStreamSrc = nval;",
            "\n", "            }",
            "\n", "            else if (nv.localeCompare(\"adbe-video-
stream-name\") == 0)",
            "\n", "            {",
            "\n", "                videoStreamName = nval;",
            "\n", "            }",
            "\n", "            else if (nv.localeCompare(\"adbe-record-
mode\") == 0)",
            "\n", "            {",
            "\n", "                recordMode = nval;",
            "\n", "            }",
            "\n", "        }",
            "\n", "    }",
            "\n", "",
            "\n", "    // exploring the object",
            "\n", "    for( var p in streamObj )",
            "\n", "{",
            "\n", "    trace( p + \": \" + streamObj[p] );",
            "\n", "}",
            "\n", "",
            "\n", "    var s = Stream.get(\"f4f:\" + streamObj.name);",
            "\n", "    if (s == undefined )",
            "\n", "        return;",
            "\n", "        ",
            "\n", "    if ((s.liveEvent != undefined)&&(s.liveEvent !=
\"\")&&(s.liveEvent != liveEventName)) {",
            "\n", "            trace(\"Rejecting publish from client:
\"+clientObj.ip +\" as stream: \"+streamObj.name+",
            "\n", "                \" is already assigned to event:
[\"+s.liveEvent +\"]\");",
            "\n", "",
            "\n", "            application.disconnect(clientObj);",
            "\n", "        ",
            "\n", "        return;",
            "\n", "    }",
            "\n", "",
            "\n", "    s.onStatus = function(info)",
            "\n", "    {",
```

```
"\n", "        this.trace(info.code);",
"\n", "    }",
"\n", "    ",
"\n", "    s.liveEvent = liveEventName;",
"\n", "    trace(\"Stream name is: \" + streamObj.name + \"
and live event is: \"+s.liveEvent);",
"\n", "    if (!s.record(recordMode))",
"\n", "    {",
"\n", "        s.trace(\"record failed.\");",
"\n", "    }",
"\n", "    ",
"\n", "    s.play(streamObj.name,-1,-1);   ",
"\n", "        ",
"\n", "           ",
"\n", "    application.s[streamObj.name] = s;",
"\n", "    ",
"\n", "    // check if audio only stream is desired",
"\n", "    if (audioStreamName != \"\")",
"\n", "    {",
"\n", "        // if no stream src specified, use this
stream",
"\n", "        if (audioStreamSrc == \"\")",
"\n", "        {",
"\n", "            audioStreamSrc = streamObj.name;",
"\n", "        }",
"\n", "        ",
"\n", "        if (audioStreamSrc == streamObj.name)",
"\n", "        {",
"\n", "            //trace(\"Creating audio only stream \"
+ audioStreamName + \" from \" + audioStreamSrc);",
"\n", "                var a = Stream.get(\"f4f:\" + audio-
StreamName);",
"\n", "            a.onStatus = function(info)",
"\n", "            {",
"\n", "                this.trace(info.code);",
"\n", "            }",
"\n", "            a.receiveAudio = true;",
"\n", "            a.receiveVideo = false;",
"\n", "            a.liveEvent = liveEventName;",
"\n", "            if (!a.record(recordMode))",
"\n", "            {",
"\n", "                a.trace(\"record failed.\");",
"\n", "            }",
"\n", "            ",
"\n", "            a.play(audioStreamSrc, -1, -1);",
"\n", "            application.a[streamObj.name] = a;",
"\n", "            ",
"\n", "        }",
"\n", "    }",
"\n", "    ",
"\n", "    // check if video only stream is desired",
"\n", "    if (videoStreamName != \"\")",
```

```
                    "\n", "    {",
                      "\n", "        // if no stream src specified, use this
stream",
                    "\n", "        if (videoStreamSrc == \"\")",
                    "\n", "        {",
                    "\n", "            videoStreamSrc = streamObj.name;",
                    "\n", "        }",
                    "\n", "    ",
                    "\n", "        if (videoStreamSrc == streamObj.name)",
                    "\n", "        {",
                      "\n", "            trace(\"Creating video only stream \" +
videoStreamName + \" from \" + videoStreamSrc);",
                      "\n", "            var v = Stream.get(\"f4f:\" + video-
StreamName);",
                    "\n", "            v.onStatus = function(info)",
                    "\n", "            {",
                    "\n", "                this.trace(info.code);",
                    "\n", "            }",
                    "\n", "            v.receiveAudio = false;",
                    "\n", "            v.receiveVideo = true;",
                    "\n", "            v.liveEvent = liveEventName;",
                    "\n", "            if (!v.record(recordMode))",
                    "\n", "            {",
                    "\n", "                v.trace(\"record failed.\");",
                    "\n", "            ",
                    "\n", "            }",
                      "\n", "                v.play(videoStreamSrc, -1,
-1);        ",
                    "\n", "            application.v[streamObj.name] = v;",
                    "\n", "        ",
                    "\n", "        }",
                    "\n", "    }",
                    "\n", "}",
                    "\n", "",
                  "\n", "application.onUnpublish = function(clientObj, stream-
Obj)",
                    "\n", "{",
                    "\n", "    trace(\"onUnpublish : \" + streamObj.name);",
                    "\n", "    ",
                    "\n", "    var s = application.s[streamObj.name];",
                    "\n", "    trace(s);",
                    "\n", "    if (s && s!= undefined)",
                    "\n", "    {",
                    "\n", "        s.record(false);",
                    "\n", "        s.play(false);",
                      "\n", "        // trying to get FMS to remove objects (we
have problems",
                    "\n", "        // re-creating streams)",
                    "\n", "        s.clear();",
                    "\n", "        s.liveEvent = \"\";",
                    "\n", "        application.s[streamObj.name] = null;",
                    "\n", "    }",
```

```
                        "\n", "    // is this the source for audio only stream?",
                        "\n", "    var a = application.a[streamObj.name];",
                        "\n", "    trace(a);",
                        "\n", "    if (a && a != undefined)",
                        "\n", "    {",
                        "\n", "         //trace(\"Removing audio only stream \" +
a.name + \" : source = \" + streamObj.name);",
                        "\n", "         a.record(false);",
                        "\n", "         a.play(false);",
                        "\n", "         a.liveEvent = \"\";",
                        "\n", "         application.a[streamObj.name] = null;",
                        "\n", "    }",
                        "\n", "    // is this the source for video only stream?",
                        "\n", "    var v = application.v[streamObj.name];",
                        "\n", "    trace(v);",
                        "\n", "    if (v && v != undefined)",
                        "\n", "    {",
                        "\n", "         //trace(\"Removing video only stream \" +
v.name + \" : source = \" + streamObj.name);",
                        "\n", "         v.record(false);",
                        "\n", "         v.play(false);",
                        "\n", "         v.liveEvent = \"\";",
                        "\n", "         application.v[streamObj.name] = null;",
                        "\n", "    }",
                        "\n", "",
                        "\n", "    streamObj.publishing = false;    ",
                        "\n", "    if (streamObj.publishingClient != undefined && ",
                        "\n", "        streamObj.publishingClient != null)",
                        "\n", "    {",
                        "\n", "         // onPublish was suspended pending comple-
tion of onUnpublish",
                        "\n", "         // call it now.",
                        "\n", "         application.onPublish(streamObj.publishing-
Client, streamObj);",
                        "\n", "         streamObj.publishingClient = null;",
                        "\n", "    }",
                        "\n", "}",
                        "\n", "",
                        "\n", "/*",
                        "\n", "* FCPublish :",
                        "\n", "* FMLE calls FCPublish with the name of the stream
whenever a new stream ",
                        "\n", "* is published. This notification can be used by
server-side action script",
                        "\n", "* to maintain list of all streams or to force FMLE
to stop publishing.",
                        "\n", "* To stop publishing, call \"onFCPublish\" with an
info object with status",
                        "\n", "* code set to \"NetStream.Publish.BadName\".",
                        "\n", "*/ ",
                        "\n", "",
                        "\n", "Client.prototype.FCPublish = function( streamname )",
```

```
                        "\n", "{",
                        "\n", "    trace(\"streamname: \" + streamname);",
                        "\n", "    ",
                         "\n", "    // setup your stream and check if you want to
allow this stream to be published",
                        "\n", "    if ( true) // do some validation here",
                        "\n", "    {     // this is optional.",
                          "\n", "          this.call(\"onFCPublish\", null, {code:
\"NetStream.Publish.Start\", description:streamname});",
                        "\n", "    }",
                        "\n", "    else",
                        "\n", "    {",
                          "\n", "          this.call(\"onFCPublish\", null, {code:
\"NetStream.Publish.BadName\", description:streamname});",
                        "\n", "    }",
                        "\n", "       ",
                        "\n", "}",
                        "\n", "",
                        "\n", "/*",
                        "\n", "* FCUnpublish :",
                         "\n", "* FMLE notifies the server script when a stream is
unpublished.",
                        "\n", "*/",
                        "\n", "",
                            "\n", "Client.prototype.FCUnpublish = function( stream-
name )",
                        "\n", "{",
                        "\n", "    // perform your clean  up",
                         "\n", "    this.call(\"onFCUnpublish\", null, {code:\"Net-
Stream.Unpublish.Success\", description:streamname});",
                        "\n", "}",
                        "\n", "",
                        "\n", "/*",
                        "\n", "* releaseStream :",
                         "\n", "* When an FMLE connection to FMS drops during a
publishing session it",
                         "\n", "* tries to republish the stream when the connection
is restored. On certain",
                         "\n", "* occasions, FMS rejects the new stream because the
server is still ",
                         "\n", "* unaware of the connection drop, sometimes this can
take a few minutes.",
                         "\n", "* FMLE calls the \"releaseStream\" method with the
stream name and this can be",
                        "\n", "* used to forcibly clear the stream.",
                        "\n", "*/ ",
                            "\n", "Client.prototype.releaseStream = function(stream-
name)",
                        "\n", "{",
                        "\n", "    var s = Stream.get(streamname);",
                        "\n", "    if (s) {",
                        "\n", "        s.play(false);",
```

```
                    "\n", "      }",
                    "\n", "}",
                    "\n", "EOF",
                    "\n", "",
                        "\n", "mkdir -p /mnt/applications/livepkgr/events/_de-
finst_/", { "Ref" : "EventName" },
                    "\n", "curl --silent \\",
                    "\n", "   https://s3-eu-west-1.amazonaws.com/cgb.video-
dock.eu/fms/applications/livepkgr/events/_definst_/", { "Ref" : "EventName" },
"/Manifest.xml | \\",
                    "\n", "   sed 's/streamname/", { "Ref" : "StreamName" },
"/' > \\",
                    "\n", "   /mnt/applications/livepkgr/events/_definst_/",
{ "Ref" : "EventName" }, "/Manifest.xml",
                    "\n", "curl --silent \\",
                    "\n", "   https://s3-eu-west-1.amazonaws.com/cgb.video-
dock.eu/fms/applications/livepkgr/events/_definst_/", { "Ref" : "EventName" },
"/Event.xml | \\",
                    "\n", "   sed 's/eventname/", { "Ref" : "EventName" }, "/'
> \\",
                    "\n", "   /mnt/applications/livepkgr/events/_definst_/",
{ "Ref" : "EventName" }, "/Event.xml",
                    "\n", "/bin/chown fmsuser.fmsgroup -R /mnt/applications",
                    "\n", "/opt/adobe/fms/fmsmgr server fms restart"
                ] ] }}
            }
        },
        "FMSOriginServerSecurityGroup" : {
            "Type" : "AWS::EC2::SecurityGroup",
            "Properties" : {
                "GroupDescription" : "Security group for live HTTP streaming using
Amazon CloudFront",
                "SecurityGroupIngress" : [
                    {"IpProtocol" : "tcp", "FromPort" : "22", "ToPort" : "22",
"CidrIp" : "0.0.0.0/0"},
                    {"IpProtocol" : "tcp", "FromPort" : "80", "ToPort" : "80",
"CidrIp" : "0.0.0.0/0"},
                    {"IpProtocol" : "tcp", "FromPort" : "1111", "ToPort" : "1111",
"CidrIp" : "0.0.0.0/0"},
                    {"IpProtocol" : "tcp", "FromPort" : "1935", "ToPort" : "1935",
"CidrIp" : "0.0.0.0/0"},
                    {"IpProtocol" : "udp", "FromPort" : "1935", "ToPort" : "1935",
"CidrIp" : "0.0.0.0/0"}
                ]
            }
        },
        "FMSDNSRecord" : {
            "Type" : "AWS::Route53::RecordSet",
            "Properties" : {
                "HostedZoneName" : "cgb.videodock.eu.",
                "Comment" : "FMS streaming entry point.",
                "Name" : { "Fn::Join" : [ "", [ { "Ref" : "EventName" }, ".cgb.video-
```

```
dock.eu" ]]},
        "Type" : "CNAME",
        "TTL" : "60",
            "ResourceRecords" : [
                {"Fn::GetAtt":["FMSOriginServer","PublicDnsName"]}
            ]
    }
},
    "CDNDNSRecord" : {
        "Type" : "AWS::Route53::RecordSet",
        "Properties" : {
            "HostedZoneName" : "cgb.videodock.eu.",
            "Comment" : "FMS streaming entry point.",
            "Name"  : { "Fn::Join" : [ "", [ "cdn.", { "Ref" : "EventName" },
".cgb.videodock.eu" ]]},
        "Type" : "CNAME",
        "TTL" : "60",
            "ResourceRecords" : [
                {"Fn::GetAtt":["LiveStreamingDistribution","DomainName"]}
            ]
    }
}
},

    "Outputs" : {
        "WowzaHostname" : {
            "Description" : "Hostname (Route53) of the Wowza instance",
            "Value" : { "Ref" : "WowzaDNSRecord" }
        },
        "FMSHostname" : {
            "Description" : "Hostname (Route53) of the FMS instance",
            "Value" : { "Ref" : "FMSDNSRecord" }
        },
        "FMSURL" : {
            "Value" : { "Fn::Join" : ["", ["rtmp://", { "Ref" : "FMSDNSRecord" }, "/
livepkgr"]] },
            "Description" : "FMS 4.5 Server Stream Publishing Location"
        },
        "Stream" : {
            "Value" : { "Fn::Join" : ["", [{ "Ref" : "StreamName" }, "?adbe-live-
event=", { "Ref" : "EventName" }, ""]] },
            "Description" : "Stream Name"
        },
        "FlashMediaPlayback" : {
            "Value" : { "Fn::Join" : ["", ["http://www.osmf.org/configurator/
fmp/"]] },
            "Description" : "Flash Media Playback Setup"
        },
        "LiveHDSManifest" : {
            "Value" : { "Fn::Join" : ["", ["http://", { "Ref" : "CDNDNSRecord" }, "/
hds-live/livepkgr/_definst_/", { "Ref" : "EventName" }, ".f4m"]] },
            "Description" : "Live HDS Manifest"
```

```
        },
        "LiveHLSManifest" : {
            "Value" : { "Fn::Join" : ["", ["http://", { "Ref" : "CDNDNSRecord" }, "/
hls-live/livepkgr/_definst_/", { "Ref" : "EventName" }, ".m3u8"]] },
            "Description" : "Live HLS Manifest"
        },
        "FMSServerAdminConsole" : {
            "Value" : { "Fn::Join" : ["", ["http://", { "Ref" : "FMSDNSRecord" }, "/
fms_adminConsole.htm"]] },
            "Description" : "FMS 4.5 Server"
        },
        "FMSAdminConsoleServerAddress" : {
            "Value" : { "Fn::Join" : ["", [ { "Ref" : "FMSDNSRecord" }, ":1111"]] },
            "Description" : "FMS Administration Console Server Address"
        }
    }
}
```

Orchestration

Wikipedia defines orchestration as follows
Orchestration is the study or practice of writing music for an orchestra
(or, more loosely, for any musical ensemble) or of adapting for orchestra
music composed for another medium. It only gradually over the course
of music history came to be regarded as a compositional art in itself.

The interesting thing about this definition is that it does not include performance. If we
talk about orchestration in a software system's context we implicitly include the art of
conducting, or performing.

Tools like puppet and chef originate from a pre-Cloud era. They focus on automating
complex stack deployment, with numerous dependencies.

In the cloud you have other tools that can alleviate much of the pain that puppet/chef
style tools aim to take away. If you can make an AMI, installing software at deploy time
is not necessary anymore. Perhaps the only thing you want to do is to get the latest
version of your own software, most of the time from a repository like github.

Many of the systems we have described so far do not require a lot of handling before
they are up and running. Chef or puppet would be unnecessary overkill and would
introduce unwanted complexity that might do more harm than good.

There is a class of problems that do require scripted orchestration. One example is the *occasional stack*. If you have a large development team, with members joining/leaving all the time, you can use CloudFormation plus Chef to spin up dev environments easily. But if you have two streaming events per month it is not very cost-effective to have a full platform all of the time.

CloudFormation (and/or Chef/Puppet) are not the easiest tools to use, especially if you rely on them in your operation and your operation requires extensive testing. Unfortunately, there is no such thing as an AWS simulator (yet), so building solutions with CloudFormation or tools like Chef or Puppet is quite time consuming. You can do the math. If it all adds up, go and have fun.

Route 53

In early 2012 AWS introduced latency-based routing. With this feature you can tell Route 53 to route users (or devices) to the closest end point (in the sense of latency). You can mix and match ELBs, EC2 instances, or A records across regions.

Moving your processing closer to the origin of the request makes sense for the origin, especially if it is a human being waiting for a page to load, but it also helps you deal with the loss of an entire Region.

Region gone missing
Missing Regions is not something that happened to our recollection. What can happen is that certain key features are not accessible. If you lose an instance and you can't launch another, you lose the Region from your point of view.

Global Database

Spanning an app across multiple Regions poses its own new set of problems. One of the most difficult to solve is a global database. There is hardly a database that can handle geographic dispersement at the continental level.

This is one area of innovation to watch—the development of simple and easy to set datastores that can handle the intricacies of long distance relationships with their peers.

Spanner
Google has published a research paper (*http://bit.ly/T9LHpZ*) on a technology they call Spanner. This new database technology aims to solve global distribution of data, while respecting certain database properties like consistency.

## CHAPTER 11

Conclusion

The general requirement of services in production is that most of the time they cannot break. We are used to the general availability of services like Gmail that are always one. We expect these services to be basically free and never break. This generally takes a lot of time and effort.

In discussing the actual definition of *cannot break* it quickly becomes clear that small interruptions are not a big problem. It is more important that it doesn't happen all the time, and that you can rely on the system to fix itself quickly. In other words the system needs to be **Reliable**.

There are many factors that can cause harm to your system. It might be a lightning strike causing power to be interrupted. Or it may be that you are nursing your newborn at night and make a sleepy mistake. Systems can be designed to withstand these events; they should be engineered for **Resilience**.

In this book we have shown how we usually design, build, and operate for **Resilience and Reliability on AWS**. The overview we have given of this platform and of the way we run our production is definitely not complete. And the examples are how we run our stuff in production. If we have inspired you to build or improve your own systems, then we have succeeded in what we set out to do.

There are certain aspects we have not touched on here. We did not overly focus on the cost of infrastructures. A good infrastructure always utilizes the minimum number of components. If you achieve this, applying principles like Reserved and Spot instances is not difficult anymore.

We are struggling day in and day out to achieve the highest levels of quality, especially in terms of Resilience and Reliability. We hope you can benefit from our struggles. May your infrastructures improve every day!

About the Authors

Jurg van Vliet graduated from the University of Amsterdam in Computer Science. After his internship with Philips Research, he worked for many web startups and media companies. Passionate about technology, he wrote for many years about it and its effects on society. He became interested in the cloud and started using AWS in 2007. After merging his former company, 2Yellows, with a research firm, he decided to start 9Apps, an AWS boutique that is an AWS solution provider and silver partner of Eucalyptus, together with Flavia. Give Jurg a scalability challenge, and he will not sleep until he solves it— and he will love you for it.

Flavia Paganelli has been developing software in different industries and languages for over 14 years, for companies like TomTom and Layar. She moved to The Netherlands with her cat after finishing an MSc in Computer Science at the University of Buenos Aires. A founder of 9Apps, Flavia loves to create easy-to-understand software that makes people's lives easier, like the Decaf EC2 smartphone app. When she is not building software, she is probably exercising her other passions, like acting or playing capoeira.

Jasper Geurtsen has been a pragmatic software developer for over 15 years. After programming embedded systems for many years, like the TomTom devices, he co-founded 9apps. This brought him into a world with an infinite supply of cloud computing resources. He loves making all kind of systems work together with other fun people. When he is not making systems work, Jasper enjoys going to music concerts, hiking, and camping with his girlfriend and their two children.

Have it your way.